COMMERCIAL FISHERMEN
GREAT LAKES STYLE

The boats, the jobs, the men and women, and their families

Bob Ojala

With Nancy Swaer

© 2023 Bob Ojala. All rights reserved. No portion of this book may be reproduced, stored in a retrieval system, or transmitted in any form or by any means—electronic, mechanical, photocopy, recording, scanning, or other— except for brief quotations in critical reviews or articles, without the prior written permission of the publisher and author.

Color 978-1-088077-78-8 Black and White 978-1-0880-8015-3 Color E-book 978-1-0881-2371-3

DEDICATION

To the fishermen and their families who keep us fed with wonderful, Great Lakes fish. The average person buying fish in their local grocery store has no idea the long hours, hard work, and dangers involved in fishing, particularly the details about the Great Lakes.
They might remember movies like the *Perfect Storm*, or TV shows like *Deadliest Catch*, but they don't know that on the night the Edmund Fitzgerald sank on Lake Superior, there were numerous Great Lakes fishermen fighting that same storm. One crew was stranded on an island in Lake Superior, but there were no fishermen's deaths…just a lot of sunken or damaged fishing tugs.

Commercial Fishing is the most dangerous profession on a worldwide basis. So, the next time you buy fish, whether it is Great Lakes caught or Deep Sea, remember what the fishermen and their families endure so that you can enjoy that fresh fish! Our Great Lakes fishing fleet is a small fraction of what it was just 50 years ago, and it is getting tougher all the time for these families to make a living.

CONTENTS

ACKNOWLEDGEMENTS	VII
BOOK COVER STORY	X
FISH OF THE GREAT LAKES	XIII
INTRODUCTION	1
HISTORY OF TWO RIVERS, WISCONSIN, FISHING	7
CEDAR RIVER, MICHIGAN FISHING FAMILIES	17
WOMEN FISHERMEN ON THE GREAT LAKES	23
SWAER FAMILY STORY	25
SWAER FAMILY ICE FISHING	49
FIRST CATCH	69
CHRIS PETERSEN	103
TWO RIVERS, WISCONSIN FISHING MUSEUM	117
JIM LEGAULT PHOTOGRAPHY	121

STORMS, WRECKS, AND DANGERS	129
LEGISLATION PROBLEMS	133
PURVIS FISHERIES	137
SHAUN VARY	143
OCONTO, WISCONSIN	147
AL STRANZ	151
ABOUT THE AUTHOR	157

ACKNOWLEDGEMENTS

I hate to leave out any important people who helped with this book. I was jumping into a subject for which I had a sincere interest and deep respect for the people who dedicated their working life to performing. But my hands-on experience was from my teen years in Marinette, Wisconsin, watching Commercial Fishermen at work. However, I've never had a problem with admitting I needed help.

Starting chronologically, Jamie LeClair at Susie-Q Fisheries in Two Rivers, Wisconsin, got me started. I had the basic ideas of what I wanted to have in the book, presenting the true-life stories of these fishermen, using as much of their actual words as possible, similar to my published book, <u>Sweetwater Sailors</u>. There were good books written *about* the sailors, but they were all in the author's words. I wanted to see one with the fishermen's words! I found out that was going to be tough. But Jamie LeClair gave me a great start, with pictures, family history, and some great stories from her dad, Mike LeClair.

Then I had some disappointments with families who were too busy to put their story together, some with health problems. What I eventually found out was that there was a fear of, I might say too much, getting them in trouble with state authorities, despite my promises to never do that.

Jamie LeClair kept me going, however. She first introduced me to Titus Seilheimer, a Ph.D. Fisheries Specialist, working with the Wisconsin Sea Grant. Titus allowed me to use some of his photos, and when I sent him a copy of my manuscript, to show him how I was using his materials, he did a great job of editing, pointing out mistakes, and adding information where I had highlighted questions. Then when I asked Jamie for more photos of the Susie-Q operation, she introduced me to Jim Legault. That explanation of Jim's photos is detailed in this book.

In the meantime, my discouragement was increasing due to numerous fishing families being polite when I contacted them, but then ignoring my reminders to put something together. Then I got lucky. I bumped into a Facebook page called Fish Tugs of the Great Lakes. Several people responded to a post I made on that page, asking for help with the book. One of them was Shaun Vary, a Great Lakes Merchant Mariner whose family were Fishermen out of Canada. He introduced me to several other contributors.

But then I got a message from Nancy Swaer, which changed everything! Nancy had fished with her father, Norbert Swaer, during her college years. She not only had actual fishing experience, but she knew her father's stories and had numerous photos. I asked Nancy whether her father had ice-fished on Green Bay during the winters, and she told me that her brothers had fished with her dad. So, she talked with her brother, Dennis Swaer, giving another abundance of details, stories, and photographs. Then Nancy contacted Al Stranz who had fished with the Moes family out of Oconto.

In addition to providing all this material for the book, Nancy did a great job of editing, not just for the Swaer sections, but for the rest of the book. She was also my beta-reader for the book, suggesting changes and finding errors and omissions. When I told Nancy that I was going to place her name under mine on the Title Page, she objected, saying she wasn't a co-author, but she was so much more than just a contributor, so I had to give her that additional credit.

Nancy & Dennis Swaer, with the author, taken in October 2022.

BOOK COVER STORY

The picture on the cover of this book shows an old wooden boat called "Snooks." It is very important to the Swaer family. The following story is from Dennis Swaer:

I was working with Dad fishing Perch and we were beginning to get alewife (we called them shad) in the gillnets. It was a real nuisance because they were difficult to remove from the nets due to the tiny spines on their bellies that angled forward. We could not just stick an awl through the eyes and pull them through the mesh the way we could with perch. They often tangled in the netting and had to be backed out. And, they were not fit for human consumption so they had little value. I remember Dad squeezing the roe out of the belly of one, remarking on how fine the eggs were and how many each fish carried. His point was that they would likely multiply quickly and in large numbers. He got the right!

After my Uncle Art Swaer built the fishmeal plant providing a market for "shad", Dad attempted to catch them by trawling with the "Casey Bros." The little Gray Marine 2-71 did not have enough power to effectively pull the trawl, so pond netting was the option he chose. I went with him to Menomonee to get net from, I believe it was a man called Angwall. An agreement was reached to use the net and to give Angwall a share. I specifically remember the trip because when we were in the twine shed selecting a net, I nearly had my head taken off for lighting a cigarette. This was tarred twine and there was quite a bit of tar-dust in the air which I was informed could explode. Lesson learned with just an explosion of the verbal variety. We, and when I say we, I mean Dad with me as a helper, set and lifted the net with the Casey Bros and a rowboat. It soon became clear that a "pond net boat" was needed.

Dad found a wooden strip boat, the Snooks, 10 or 15 miles from Pensaukee, up the west shore of the Bay of Green Bay on the bank of the Suamico River. I don't recall if it had a nonfunctional engine or no engine. He bought it and made a plan to tow it to Pensaukee with the Casey Bros. It had been on the river bank for quite some time, allowing the wood of the hull to dry and shrink. It would surely have leaked like a sieve if launched outright. For several days water was pumped into the hull while the Snooks was on shore allowing the wood to soak and swell. Eventually she was launched and still leaked, but could be kept afloat with a sump pump.

We took the Casey Bros to Suamico along with a tow line, a submersible electric pump and a long extension cord. The "light plant" in Casey Bros. was powered by a Briggs and Stratton engine and turned a generator that produced 110 volts AC current for the pump. The tow line was attached, extension cord suspended from another line between the two boats, and the light plant fired up.

All worked well, so we headed down river to the deeper water of the Bay and set course for Pensaukee, with Dad in the Casey Bros. and me in the Snooks monitoring the pump.

All was fine for a while until the bilge water started getting deeper, even though the pump was still running. As the situation seemed to be getting worse, I signaled Dad to let him know I was losing the battle with the water level. It became apparent that if things continued the way they were going, the Snooks would fill with water and likely sink before we made port. He changed course for shore so that the seemingly inevitable would happen in shallower water.

Even though the pump was running, I discovered the intake was getting partly clogged with debris from the bilge. As we proceeded toward beaching the Snooks, I was able to unclog the intake, reorient the pump, and place it on a board that prevented the debris from entering directly. I signaled Dad and let him know that we were now holding our own with the water level and eventually making some progress. Again, we set course for Pensaukee, staying as close to shore as the water depth allowed.

We made it. And now the Snooks will be on the cover of this book!

FISH OF THE GREAT LAKES

Natural to the Great Lakes

Lake Whitefish (and other varieties)
Walleye
Yellow Perch
White Perch
Brown Trout
Lake Trout
Rainbow Trout
Steelhead (hybrid rainbow)
Brook Trout
Muskellunge (Muskie)
Pickerel (varieties)
Northern Pike
Lake Sturgeon
Bluegill
Smelt
Herring
Chubs (varieties)
Crappie
Carp (not Asian Carp)
Suckers
Bullhead (varieties)
Catfish
American Eel
Shiner (varieties)
Shad
Redhorse
Dace (varieties)
Darter
Drum (Sheepshead)
Striped Bass
White Bass
Small Mouth Bass
Large Mouth Bass
Sauger gar
Warmouth
Bowfin
Fall Fish

Planted and Invasive

Salmon (all varieties)
Alewife
Lamprey
Goby

And no, there are no sharks, tuna, swordfish, shrimp, scallops, etc. in Great Lakes waters!

INTRODUCTION

After the publication of the first Sweetwater Sailors book, I realized that we had ignored, though unintentionally, a very important, and very interesting segment of the Great Lakes maritime community: Commercial Fishermen.

Everyone interested in the Great Lakes is aware of the tragic sinking of the S.S. *Edmund Fitzgerald* in November 1975. But how many people realize that numerous commercial fishing vessels sank during that storm and that one fish-tug crew was stranded on an island during that storm? One of the first vessels to search for *Fitzgerald* survivors that night was a Great Lakes Commercial Fishing tug. These sailors are experienced, tough mariners, but few people even know that they exist. I hope enough people read this book to better appreciate them.

This author grew up in Marinette, Wisconsin, and the Menekaunee Harbor area of the Menominee River, as well as Peshtigo Harbor, were well known to me. I had known numerous commercial fishermen, and my mother and her sister were friends of several of their families. Therefore, I'm surprised that I overlooked these fishing families.

In my home area, located on Green Bay, those fishermen continued to fish once the Bay had frozen over, driving trucks out onto the ice to set their gill nets. I even had two small, 50-foot gill nets myself, which I set through the ice when I was a young teen. One of my mother's sisters also dated a commercial fisherman from the Peshtigo Harbor area, and we always enjoyed a regular supply of fresh fish, including Lawyer livers, which my mother and my aunt enjoyed (not me).

Commercial Fishing has probably been around since the first European settlers arrived on the Great Lakes, and Native Americans may have shown some of those settlers how to fish in these freshwater lakes. However, many settlers came from fishing families back in Europe, so they probably brought some of their methods with them. Early Lake Michigan fishermen used seine and trawler net methods, pond (pound) nets, and hoop nets before the gill nets came into use.

I realized my omission one day when I stopped in my favorite Great Lakes fish market in Two Rivers, Wisconsin. I had been shopping for my fresh fish at SUSIE-Q Fisheries in Two Rivers ever since the late 1970s, because of my frequent trips to Bay Shipbuilding in Sturgeon Bay. I preferred the "scenic route" through Algoma and Kewaunee, along Lake Michigan, and found SUSIE-Q while driving through Two Rivers. My family always loved their fresh fish and the variety of smoked fish available, particularly their smoked chubs.

INTRODUCTION

During that recent stop for three whole whitefish (always best when cooked on the bone), I picked up a brochure on their counter. When I returned home, I sent an email to their general email address, telling them about my intended project. I was pleased to get a quick return message from Jamie LeClair, stating she was the sixth generation of the LeClair family (origins from Louis Clair Houde, who brought Charles LeClair to Two Rivers). They then changed the name to LeClair, fishing in the Two Rivers area, (sixth generation, if the first, non-fishermen are included) and Jamie said she had a lot of information she was willing to share. Jamie also directed me to the Rogers Street Fishing Village in Two Rivers, and I also met with Jamie's father, Mike LeClair, the primary captain and current owner of the company.

The interest from the LeClair family encouraged me to place a post on the Facebook page, Menekaunee Memories, where I had seen numerous posts about the fishing fleet in that area. Again, I was surprised by the prompt responses from several of the followers of that group, who gave me names and contact information for people to contact. One person in particular, Karen Petersen, said that her family, the Andersons, had fished out of the Bark River, Michigan, area, and Karen also knew Noreen Johnson, the curator of the West Shore Fishing Museum. We soon arranged a great meeting at that museum to discuss the project.

INTRODUCTION

My next visit was with Paul Brunette, from a fishing family out of Pensaukee, Wisconsin. I had met Paul several years earlier when I surveyed one of his fish tugs, which was being sold to a new owner, to be used as a pleasure vessel. We had a meeting with Paul, his brother, Dan, and another retired fisherman who was a friend of the Brunettes.

Several more fishermen or their families have contacted me from Lakes Erie, Huron, and Lake Superior, wishing to include their unusual stories.

So, these first contacts have led to this very interesting collection of stories about the Great Lakes commercial fishing industry. I've tried to use the first-hand stories I received directly from the fishermen, as much as possible.

HISTORY OF TWO RIVERS, WISCONSIN, FISHING

As detailed in the book, Neshotah: the story of Two Rivers, Wisconsin, the LeClair family moved to Two Rivers, Wisconsin, from Canada in 1845-46, after a short stop in Chicago. Charles LeClair first started lumbering before getting into fishing. His two sons, Nelson and David continued the family's fishing tradition, and were credited with the technique of fishing, using the "pond net," also referred to as the pound net. The LeClairs also built their own ice houses, collecting ice during the winter, and fish sheds to store their nets and rigs out of the weather. In 1880, Two Rivers had the largest fleet of Mackinaw boats on Lake Michigan, selling much of their catch in the Chicago markets. The next generation, Norbert and George Le Clair continued fishing, and a novel by George Vukelich, Fishermen's Beach, was based upon the George LeClair family.

I wanted some good current pictures of the fishermen and their catches, but as I was told by more than one fisherman, "If I'm taking pictures, I'm not catching fish." However, Jamie LeClair put me in touch with Titus Seilheimer, a Ph.D. Fisheries Specialist, working with the Wisconsin Sea Grant. Titus and his crew spent about 125 days out on the *"Peter Paul"* with the LeClairs, and Titus graciously allowed me to use many of their photos in this book. Therefore, all of the color photos in this section were taken by the Wisconsin Sea Grant crew. Thank you, Titus!

I asked Jamie LeClair, who is the sixth generation of the family in the Two Rivers area, to ask her father, Mike LeClair, to jot down some of his memories about the family's fishing history in the Two Rivers area. The following memories and experiences were provided by Mike LeClair:

"In 1962, my father, Pete LeClair, and his partner, Bill Kunesh (from the Marinette area), purchased the *Avis J* boat from Lake Erie. They converted it from a gill net boat to a trawler. They started out trawling for chubs, but alewife showed up in Lake Michigan, so they began fishing for them. It became a very large industry. Two Rivers had seven trawlers in the mid-70s and were catching 40 to 50 million pounds per year. The alewives were used for pet food and fish meal. (Per Sea Grant, Alewife had been around in smaller numbers, but as other small fish like chubs and herring declined, the alewife increased. The opening of the St. Lawrence Seaway also allowed more alewife to reach the Great Lakes.)

"My grandfather, Joe LeClair, had the *Susie-Q* built at Schwarz Marine in Two Rivers. My dad became good friends with Bernard Schwarz. Schwarz Marine needed to deliver one of the boats they had constructed to Chicago. Schwartz and my father left the Two Rivers harbor and got just south of Manitowoc when the boat was observed by the Coast Guard in Two Rivers going in circles. They dispatched a rescue boat and got on board the vessel. They found my father and Schwarz passed out. They started CPR on Schwarz because he was still breathing. My dad was not breathing. There was a guy from the Coast Guard standing there watching, and the person in charge told him he might as well try to revive my dad, and luckily it worked. The Coast Guard determined it was carbon monoxide poisoning. The engine manufacturer had used brass bolts to fasten the exhaust, and when the engine got hot, the bolts expanded and became loose, leaking exhaust into the boat.

"In the 1950s and early 60s, there were 4 or 5 car ferries running from Manitowoc to Ludington. At that time, commercial fishing boats had no radar or ship-to-shore radios, and on foggy days the fisherman couldn't see if the car ferries were close to them. One day my father was standing by the lifter door, lifting gill nets, when he heard the car ferry's horn. He knew the car ferry was close, so he began watching carefully. He then saw the large black vessel come out of the fog, heading right at him. He immediately put the *Susie-Q* in reverse, full throttle. The Car Ferry smashed into the bow of the Susie-Q. If he had not backed up, the car ferry would have cut them in half. Luckily, there were no injuries. Just a lot of damage to the bow of the Susie-Q. A few months later, our neighbor Frank Kulpa, owner of the *Bossier Brothers*, was also hit by a car ferry.

"Back in the 50s, the DNR wardens and commercial fishermen were at odds. This was because commercial fishermen were using smaller mesh-size nets than was legal to be used. The DNR had a boat called the *Barney Divine*. This boat was used to lift commercial fishermen's nets and to check their boats. My grandfather, Joe, while fishing one day, was seen by the wardens on the *Barney Divine*. The DNR tried to board the *Susie-Q* while on Lake Michigan. The day was very cold and a little rough. My grandfather told the wardens to wait until they got to the dock. The young warden, Don Euers, didn't listen and jumped onto the *Susie-Q* boat. He wanted to get inside, but my grandfather refused. The warden kicked in the window in the pilot house trying to get in, but my grandpa went after him with a gaff hook. When the warden couldn't get in, he took off his jacket and stuffed it in the exhaust thinking he would stop the engine. My grandfather opened up the throttle and his jacket went up in flames. Meanwhile, the warden is on top of the boat, waves are breaking over the boat, and it's freezing. Ice is forming on the warden and he starts begging my grandfather to let him in, telling him they won't give him a citation. My grandfather let him in, but when he got to the dock, there were wardens and police there. They went to court and the judge didn't have any sympathy for the warden. The judge only gave my grandfather a $100 fine.

"Another time, while gill netting on the *Susie-Q*, my father had four men on the boat. One older guy, two younger kids right out of high school, and himself. While lifting the gill nets, a large log became entangled in the nets. They couldn't get it out, but the older fishermen thought he could get it out by going on the roof of the boat. He was going to show the young guys how to do it. While up on the roof, a large wave hit the side of the boat and the log fell out of the nets. The old guy,

Cully Pilon, got hooked by a branch on the log and went down with the log. Everyone was scrambling to the doors of the boat to see if he'd come up. After a couple of minutes, the log must have slowed his descent so he could unhook himself, and he finally returned to the surface. He lived, but his ears were ringing years later, and he also quit fishing that year.

"I remember years ago when the ice on Lake Michigan was thick. Commercial fishing boats would have to follow the car ferries' tracks in order to get to their nets, which were 15 miles or more out from the ports. I remember my father telling me the ice was so thick that one of the fishermen walked on the ice from his boat to my father's boat when they were about 13 miles offshore.

"The fish tug, *Avis-J*, was the largest and most powerful boat in Two Rivers back in the middle 1960s. Large oil tankers used to come into Two Rivers harbor and unload fuel oil and gas. One day, there were high winds coming from the southeast and the tanker missed the pier opening, running aground north of the pier. The Coast Guard asked if we could help pull the tanker off. My dad went out with the *Avis-J* and tried to help. Frank Kulpa was on board, and he was trying to get a rope or cable to the tanker to pull on. When they got a cable attached, they tried to pull, but then a large wave came over the stern. Because they were pulling so hard on the tanker, the stern of the *Avis-J* sank. Thankfully, one of the men cut the tow rope, otherwise, the *Avis-J* would have sunk entirely. The next day, a tug came from Sturgeon Bay to pull the tanker free.

"I'm sure there are many other stories like this that happened to other commercial fishermen, but with improved electronics and better boats, safety is much better."

Al Stranz commented on Mike LeClair's story about the DNR boat as follows:

"The 'Barney Devine' was a WDNR research and enforcement boat for years. It was a Burger boat from Manitowoc, originally a commercial fishing tug. I rode on it a time or two in the early 80s. The Barney was converted back to a commercial boat by new owners and is, or was on Lake Superior in Port Wing, Cornucopia, or Bayfield. I saw it up there maybe 10-12 years ago, the owner let me take a look through it."

DANGERS

Some of Mike LeClair's memories reminded me of the fish tug, *"Linda E"*, which was struck by a tanker on Lake Michigan. There was blame on both sides, but the *Linda E* went down with all hands onboard. The tanker was not aware that they had struck the *"Linda E"*, so the vessel went undiscovered, until a Navy ship which happened to be visiting the Great Lakes, used its sonar to locate the fish tug.

I happened to get involved in the investigation, because I had surveyed the tanker, for unrelated reasons, shortly after the accident had occurred. My photographs and report from that inspection were used as evidence for the accident investigation and lawsuits.

For another story about a tragic loss of life on a Great Lakes fishing tug, see the story about the **Aletha B.** in the section written by Shaun Vary, a great historian of Canadian, Great Lakes fish tugs.

CEDAR RIVER, MICHIGAN FISHING FAMILIES

Information on the Anderson Family was obtained from Karen Petersen, from Cedar River, Michigan. Karen wrote several articles about commercial fishermen in that locale, including the Norwegian immigrant family of Even and Engberg Nelson. They emigrated to New York in 1846, and eventually settled near Green Bay, Wisconsin, in 1852. They then moved north into Door County, settling in Fish Creek and Ephraim, where they started farming and fishing. Some of the children from that family eventually married and settled in the Menominee and Carney, Michigan, area.

Another Nelson family, Andrew and Ingbor, Nelson also immigrated to the United States through Canada, at Port Huron, MI, in 1857, settling in the Fish Creek/Egg Harbor area of Door County, Wisconsin. Two of their sons served in the Union Navy during the Civil War, and one of those sons, John Nelson, married in 1878 and moved to Ingallston, Michigan, where they started a cooper's business and also started fishing. They eventually returned to Sturgeon Bay.

Tom Nelson, son of Andrew and Ingbor, married Torena Nelson, daughter of Even and Engberg Nelson, in 1867. They had four children before Tom drowned in Green Bay waters in November 1876, while trying to reposition his fishing boat during a storm. Torena was remarried to Martin Forswold in 1882.

Ida Nelson, the eldest daughter of Tom and Torena, had lived in Ingallston, Michigan with her Uncle John and Aunt Sophia Nelson after her father died. Gustie Nelson was 8 years old when her father drowned. She married, divorced, and eventually moved to Cedar River, MI, in 1908, where she also started a fishing business.

Some of the very interesting things learned from Karen Petersen's articles were from two maps, showing the fishing families located in Door County, Wisconsin, during the 1850s and 1860s, and then a map of the Ingallston Township in Michigan, directly across the waters of Green Bay in the 1870s. The Nelsons, Weborgs, and Baileys from Door County started the four original fishing businesses located in Ingallston, MI. Apparently, part of the reason for moving across Green Bay to Michigan can be explained due to the prevailing Westerly winds, which made for calmer waters on the Western Shore of the Bay. There are also better harbors on that Michigan shoreline, well suited for safely mooring the fishing boats.

ROBERT RULEAU

After placing a post on the Facebook page of the Great Lakes Fish Tugs, I was contacted by Robert Ruleau of Ruleau Brothers Company, wanting to discuss my proposed book about Great Lakes commercial fishing. He said he was the seventh-generation fisherman in his family. I had hoped to meet with Robert to obtain first-hand stories about his family's long history in commercial fishing on Lake Michigan. However, due to Robert's declining health, we were never able to get together. Robert passed away in late 2022.

The photos below are of a good catch on Robert's trawler.

A nice catch of whitefish on Green Bay

Robert's modern fish tug, trawler

With Robert's permission, I have attempted to give some history of the Rouleau family, based on articles found on the Internet.

The Ruleau ancestors

Robert sells a lot of whitefish to the Kosher food markets in New York

Robert Ruleau's family was descended from the Williams family, who had fished on Lake Michigan for over 170 years. Robert's great-grandfather, Schuyler Williams, moved to the west shore of Green Bay in about

1920. At one time, Ruleau's fishing company employed over 100 people and was producing 50 million pounds of fish per year.

Robert attended food product shows in Boston and other East Coast locations. This led to his association with several kosher food buyers, which became a major part of his business, both for fresh fish and smoked fish products.

In July 2019, Robert published an article, in several Great Lakes area newspapers, outlining the decline of commercial fishing on the Great Lakes. Robert stated that his family fished on Lake Michigan for over 170 years, and had once employed over 100 people. As of 2019, they only had 15 employees, which Robert blamed on the overregulation by the DNR, as well as the invasive species (including the planted salmon). The only viable fish left for commercial fishermen in Michigan is the whitefish.

Salmon were originally planted in various Great Lakes tributaries to handle the alewife, an invasive species. The salmon did a great job of controlling the alewife but then began to eat the smelt, chubs, and perch. The sport fishing industry which spawned from the planted salmon began to lobby the various states to protect the salmon. In the meantime, commercial fishing licenses were drastically reduced to pacify the sport fishing industry. Now, some varieties of salmon have been able to spawn in Great lakes Rivers, yet the states are still harvesting salmon roe and hatching the salmon to be planted in Great Lakes rivers. (Howard Tanner, the man behind the salmon stocking program in Michigan, said that the planting of salmon was to create a sport fishing industry, knowing that the alewife would be a good food source for the salmon.)

THE BOATS

In the early days, the boats were flat-bottomed pond boats and narrow, pointed Mackinaw boats, powered by oars or sails. The Mackinaws would set and lift four or five boxes of gill nets, approximately 1200 feet each, on an average day. Modern, diesel-powered fish tugs set and lift ten to fifteen boxes of nets each day.

Photo of open boat at West Shore Museum

The oar and sail-powered vessels were eventually replaced by steam engines, and then gas and diesel engines. The Kahlenberg family installed their first gasoline-powered marine engine in 1899, and this allowed the new, covered-cabin gill net boats to be moored upriver because they could break the ice in the river to leave the harbor.

WOMEN FISHERMEN ON THE GREAT LAKES

Trygvie Jensen wrote a wonderful book, Wooden Boats and Iron Men, (Paisa [Alt] Publishing Company) which tells the history of Commercial Fishing in Northern Lake Michigan and Door County from 1850 to 2005. I contacted Tryg after finding his book, and he graciously gave me permission to reference his stories in my own project.

One particular section in Chapter-13 of Tryg's book caught my attention, Robbie Kodanko & the Fisher Women of Sister Bay. Apparently, two women cousins, Elaine Johnson and Gretna Johns, decided that setting and lifting fish nets was not just for men, so they started fishing lake perch near Sister Bay, in Door County, WI, using a small, borrowed skiff and a 5-HP outboard motor. Their friend, Robbie Kodanko, took them to Washington Island, where they bought a few gill nets and other necessary equipment. They cut the 1200-foot gill nets in half to make them easier to handle.

Photo by Jim Legault

You will also find mention of some women fishermen in the FIRST CATCH chapter of this book, regarding subsistence fishing allowed by Native American women in Reservation waters.

SWAER FAMILY STORY

Nancy Swaer also saw the post I had made on the *Great Lakes Fish Tugs* Facebook page and contacted me about the book. Nancy's family were commercial fishermen on Green Bay, fishing out of Pensaukee, Wisconsin. As a "small world" circumstance, I happened to have surveyed one of their boats, the "*Casey Bros*." (photo below from my survey) for a potential buyer, and Nancy also saw that picture in one of my Facebook posts. Although it needed a paint job, the tug was still in good structural condition. Nancy supplied most of the following history:

The *Casey Bros* was built in 1946 at Marinette Marine for Adson Casey, Fairport, MI, equipped with a Chrysler Crown marine gas engine (later converted to diesel). In 1949, the boat was sold to Frank Gudwer, Brampton, Mich. Gudwer then sold her to Norbert Swaer, Pensaukee, WI, in 1952. Nancy was just a year old at that time.
The *Casey Bros* is now owned by Bret VanNulan, who is renovating it as a pleasure boat.

Nancy's family started fishing on the Great Lakes when her great, great-grandfather, Fredrick Rost, came to the U.S. from Germany in the 1850s. He fished out of Little Suamico, Wisconsin. His daughter, Frances, married

Charles Henry Schwer (the original surname). That name was later changed to the current spelling of Swaer. They had three sons, Joseph, Charles, and Edward. Edward Charles Swaer, pictured below, was Nancy's paternal grandfather. He started the family's first commercial fishing business in the 1920s along with his son, Art. The business was named E.C. Swaer and Son. Art's son, Dean, was the last to own and operate the family business.

Ed Swaer-founder of E.C. Swaer & Son (Art)

Art Swaer

Dean Swaer (Art's son and last owner)

Nancy's father, Norbert Swaer, and three of the other brothers, Raymond, Francis, and Clarence (Ike) continued as commercial fishermen. Ike lived and fished out of Garden, MI, but the others fished out of Pensaukee. Early on, Nancy's parents lived in Garden, MI, for a time, and her dad fished there. That was before Nancy was born. His wood fish tug at that time was called *"The Bob."* He bought the *"Casey Bros."* in 1952, which had been burned inside, and towed it up the Pensaukee River using the

Bob, where he and her mother had purchased a piece of property along the river. He then replaced the gasoline engine in the *Casey Bros*. with the diesel engine from the *Bob*.

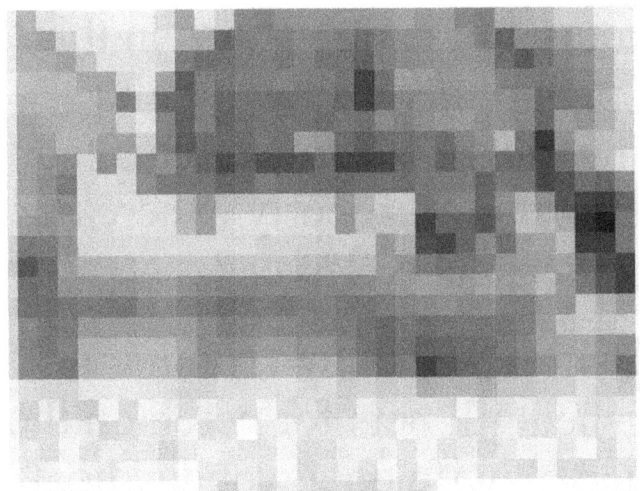 

Most of her dad's fishing years were based in Pensaukee, and their family home is still located upriver, a short distance from the bay. Nancy's brother, Dennis, now owns it, but his main residence is in Idaho, and he only spends time at the Pensaukee home a couple of times each year.

Norbert also fished out of other ports at various times while living in Pensaukee, depending upon the supply of fish, including Kewaunee and Sheboygan, WI.

Nancy provided all of the photos and explanations in this chapter (that is Nancy in the picture here, showing the *Casey Bros.* during its working days). Nancy commented, "It was docked in my dad's slip at our property, where our family home is located on the Pensaukee River."

As Nancy told me, "I fished with Dad for two summers while going to college. We fished gill nets for perch on the *Casey Brothers*. We also fished alewife on a wooden boat named '*The Snooks*'. We fished for alewife early to mid-summer until the alewife stopped spawning, and they were no longer as prevalent in the bay." See the section on *invasive species*, for more about alewife.

"We then fished gill nets on the *Casey Brothers* for perch the remainder of the summer. I had to quit in the fall to return to school, but Dad continued throughout the fall.

I fished with my dad in the summers of 1971 and 1972. My dad also fished with gill nets in the winter through the ice for whitefish as well as perch (that section provided by Dennis Swaer, later in this chapter). Then after the ice went out of the river and Green Bay, he fished for whitefish in the spring on the *Casey Brothers*."

Although there were women fishermen back in the 1800s, and then Elaine Johnson and Gretna Johns, who fished out of Door County in the early 1900s, there are only a few younger women who spent time out on the fish tugs. So, Nancy Swaer can count herself amongst the few that did.

Nancy provided the photo on the left below, which was taken by the DNR and was included in one of their magazines. She was a bit of a novelty as a woman working in an atypical job. Nancy said that the scarf she was wearing kept the fish scales out of her hair!

The second picture above shows Pensaukee Harbor in 1979, which shows Nancy's uncle, Art Swaer's fish processing plant, where the alewife was processed into fish meal as a protein source for cat food, as well as turkey and chicken feed. Nancy was also told that the oil from the fish was used for tanning leather and as an ingredient in oil-based paints. The alewife fish meal plant pictured above was in operation from 1966 -1984. Nancy continued, "The two far left boats are Art's trawlers. He usually had five, sometimes seven that trawled on Green Bay, and also on Lake Michigan and Lake Erie. My cousin Dean, Art's son, took that photo when there was a big influx of perch in Green Bay. So, fishermen came from various areas and docked there. I was no longer fishing with my dad at that time.

"I had gotten married in November 1972, then started my career as an art teacher in the Green Bay School System from which I retired after 33 years of teaching art at the middle and high school levels. My married name was Mocco for many years but is now Swaer again.

"Upriver from the view in that photo on Fish House Road was another branch of the business, E.C Swaer and Son, where they processed the local fishermen's catches. They sold filleted, smoked, and pickled fish. My mother worked there for a time filleting perch. Dean Swaer, Art's son, worked for the company and then became its owner in 1983. He also owned Schilling Fish Market in Green Bay.

"The photo below shows one of the five trawlers that my uncle owned. All were named Art Swaer in numerical order. This trawler in the photo is now owned and operated by John Kulpa Sr., the only commercial fisherman still fishing out of Pensaukee. He also owns all of the property where the vacant alewife plant is located. The plant has not been functional since 1984. There is a small marina currently behind the plant."

ALEWIFE FISHING

Those readers who lived around the Great Lakes during the 1970s and 80s will certainly remember the smell of rotting alewife along the shoreline. The salmon were planted in the Great Lakes, which eventually took care of the problem, but now we have the salmon to thank for other fishery problems (I'd better not go there!). In Lake Huron, where the alewife population has all but disappeared, the number of Chinook Salmon has also declined because alewife is their exclusive prey. Lake Michigan has more salmon because other than the

Chinook, the salmon have started feeding on the round goby as prey.

However, the commercial fishermen used the alewife as a resource when they were in abundance, processing them for their oil (used in paints) and the meal was used for cattle and pet food. The Swaer family took full advantage of the abundant alewife as explained by Nancy Swaer. But because the alewife only garnered about 2 cents per pound, that industry died as alewife populations declined.

This picture is a painting done by Nancy Swaer, showing her father, Norbert, pulling a pond net, also called "bagging the net." That was done to compact the alewife so that Nancy could drop her side net down and pull the fish into the boat.

Nancy explained, "In this photo, you can see me pulling up the alewife (we called them Shad) from a side net that dropped down into the pond net. I had to use my full weight and all my strength since it could be up to 150

lbs. of fish at a time. A two-block pulley system made it possible for me to lift that much with each pull. I filled the back area of the boat, which could be up to 5-thousand pounds per load, and we hauled two to three loads into the processing plant per day depending on how full the pond nets were. We fished three pond nets (some call them pound nets) in various locations. We took in about a million pounds of alewife one of those summers, according to my dad's records. I really developed some muscles, and I have pretty much retained good strength all of my life, probably because of those early strenuous years."

The photos above show Norbert Swaer, Nancy's father, drinking coffee and holding his pipe (he always had a pipe, which you even saw in Nancy's painting), on the way out into Green Bay to start his fishing day on the pond net boat, *The Snooks*. The other photo shows Nancy's mother, Margaret, who was actively involved in the shoreside part of the fishing business but did not go fishing (she suffered from seasickness, which I can understand). Margaret worked in the local fish house early on, but then worked as a Produce Manager in a grocery store in nearby Oconto. This picture shows her on a day she was invited along, so she could see what Norbert and Nancy were doing when fishing for alewife. Nancy said, "She even tried her hand at pulling up the side net, but she was a petite woman, and she found out it took more strength than she could muster."

Nancy explained, "This is a photo of a pond net. It had net walls that were kept vertical, using wooden stakes (usually slender tree trunks). It also had a bottom. There was a lead net that extended outward from the 'pot'. The fish would follow that lead into what was called the 'heart'. Once they swam into the heart, it directed them into the pot, where they couldn't swim back out. That's when the pond net would fill up with fish and we would harvest them from the pot."

"Both of my older brothers, Dennis and David, also worked with my dad at various times. Before the sons were old enough to work with him, he had some hired hands off and on.

"David also had his own gill net boat for a couple of years, named the '*Ion*.' He worked with dad for more years than I did, as he stayed in the area longer. My brother, Dennis, worked with Dad while he was in high school and also during summer vacations while going to college. He also did some ice fishing with him in winters."

"My dad had a new alewife boat built in 1973, called '*Snooks II*.' It was made of steel, and it was larger than '*Snooks I*'. It was a sturdier craft compared to the old wooden *Snooks* that I worked on. He also added motorization to the side drop net which made it much easier to pull the fish into the boat."

"They installed a new mechanized system, shown above being operated by Dave Swaer. However, it was still a very labor-intensive job… especially when unloading the fish into a conveyor from the stern of the boat at the fish plant."

Sorting other fish out of the alewife catch

The Swaer fish meal plant in Pensaukee

Conveyor from boats into the plant

The boiler for "cooking" alewife into fish meal

The "cooker" (smelled terrible!)

Pile of completed fish meal

GILL NET FISHING

Dave Swaer's Gill Net boat

Nephew Ryan Sohnweide

"In later years, my nephew, Ryan, also worked with his grandfather, Norbert, for three summers on the *Casey Bros.*, fishing gill nets. He is pictured above with a box of perch. You can see the typical row of boxes of gill nets along the side bench after the fish were "picked" out of them. They were also lined up that way for setting.

This photo shows Ryan as a child, with his Uncle Dave Swaer, laying out gill nets to dry on the lawn, next to Norbert's shanty, where Norbert strung up and mended his nets. That shanty was often the gathering place for the local, Pensaukee fishermen.

Lifter, pulling Gill Nets

Nets Perch in a Gill Net

"This is a photo of my uncle, Francis Swaer, next to his boat, the *"Regina."* It was taken at his dock, which was adjacent to my father's land. The *Regina* was named after his mother (my grandmother) Nellie Regina Swaer. She was born in 1880 and died in 1984, so she lived to be 104. Her husband, Ed Swaer, started the fishing business of E.C. Swaer and Son. He passed away when my father was only 17. My grandmother never remarried. Uncle Francis' son, Ed, also did some commercial fishing with the Regina, but only part-time, as he also worked for the County."

UNUSUAL MEMORIES

I asked Nancy to share some of her unusual memories from the time she was fishing with her father. I think the following experiences are amazing, for the short time Nancy was fishing, they show just how unusual the life of a Commercial Fisherman/woman can be:

- "I wore heavy yellow oil pants and thick rubber boots because I was standing/walking in the stern of the boat in fish up to and sometimes over my knees. The alewife was much easier to pull in the boat with the net I dropped down if they were alive. In the photo below, you can see the lively fish flipping around. However, if for some reason, usually, weather related, they had to be left in the pond nets longer than normal, then they would die in the nets. It was extremely hard to lift them into the boat because they were dead

weight. It was also very hard shoveling them into the conveyor once we were at the fish plant."

- "One day I had some bad luck. As I was walking out to the boat in the morning, an overhead seagull pooped on me. When we were out by the nets, I leaned back onto the boat rail and a bee stung me in the hand. Later that day, a bullhead's side stinger went through my boot. I was quite ready to go home by that time. I now laugh to myself about that day. But it didn't seem so funny at the time."

- "One Friday, a storm was rolling in quickly when we were out at a pond net and the boat was partially filled with alewife. We quickly undid everything and headed for the fish plant. I sat in the large door opening in front of the plant as the storm was passing through. All of a sudden, lightning struck the tall antenna on one of my uncle's trawlers that were docked there … not far from me. It sounded like a gun had been fired right next to my head. It frayed out the antenna to look like a broom. Not long after that, I think it was the following week, another storm hit and I was in the same location. Lightning struck yet another antenna, as they were so high up in the air. That time it melted the antenna down and started a fire inside the wheelhouse."

o "My dad and I left very early in the morning on the *Casey Bros.* and we would head to where the gill nets were set, sometimes an hour out. On the way there, I would sleep on an old mattress up in the bow of the boat. On the way back home, Dad would sleep in the bow until we got into the river, and then he needed to dock the boat. I had to wake him because I wasn't able to dock a 35-foot steel boat (not sure what would have happened to the dock if I had tried!) I never did dock his boat. I now have my own 21-foot pleasure boat that I pilot and dock myself at a marina in Green Bay, and it's still a bit unusual to see women running a boat, even these days. Even most pleasure boats are piloted by men."

o "We experienced some very rough waters on Green Bay with the *Casey Brothers*. I remember sometimes having to close up all of the doors and hatches to keep the water from splashing in. The *Casey Bros.* rolled quite well. I never had a problem with seasickness, and actually really liked it when it got rough. It was exciting to me.

I also liked it if a large ship was going across our path on the Bay, leaving a large wake."

- o "The conveyor seen in the boat photos was used to get the fish out of the boat at the processing plant. It fed into another larger conveyor at the fish plant dock, which dropped the fish into the back of a dump truck. The dump truck was then driven inside the fish plant. A very physical part of my job, as well as Dad's, was to shovel those boatloads of fish onto that conveyor. If the fish had died in the nets for some reason, it made it even harder."

- o "I've always loved seagulls and have done paintings of them. I loved throwing scraps of fish to them when they came in a big flock when we were lifting the gill nets.  They would land on the top of the boat and leave white streaks as they left – as you can see in the photo of the *Casey Bros*. We fondly called them 'Norbert's Chickens'. This is one of my paintings, 'Curious Gull' (Oil, 16 x 20 inches)."

o"My father's shanty, which was on our property next to the river, and adjacent to our family home, was the gathering place of the town's fishermen. They visited, talked about their catches, and played cards. I loved watching my dad string nets, and in cold weather, he had a big old wood-burning stove that would keep it nice and cozy. He always smoked a pipe and I can still see the red can of Union Leader from which he loaded it. He quit in later years. My Dad was a very easy-going man and everyone liked him, which is why they gathered in his shanty."

o"Dad did not initially go into commercial fishing. He went to Badger Business College in Green Bay after graduating from high school. He earned a degree in accounting and worked for a short time as a billing clerk. But he decided that he preferred fishing, and he purchased his first fishing license in 1939. In his late 30s, he was also employed as a marine engineer on landing craft built in Kewaunee and Sturgeon Bay, then transported through the Erie Canal and down the Atlantic coast to the Carolinas. I remember him being gone a lot during that time and we missed him."

o"My dad was also a self-taught musician who played the guitar, mandolin, and organ. He taught both of his sons to play the guitar, which they carried on throughout their lives. They both were in rock bands in their early years. Our family was very musical, and at family gatherings, they would sing along while Norbert, Dennis, Dave, and son-in-law Reg would all play guitar. Dad loved playing games and we often played cribbage. In his later years, he also loved to play golf."

o "A typical sight when I was growing up were net reels along the banks of the Pensaukee river. Many of the commercial fishing families had reels on their properties. Below is a photo of my siblings, Dennis and Carol as children, pulling the dried nets off of the reels in our backyard. I think they got a small allowance for their work. I used to fill what were called "needles" with the nylon that my dad used to mend nets. I think I got a nickel for each one filled.

I saved two needles fully filled. (pen is to show size)"

There was a great article published in a Green Bay newspaper in 1984, describing the career of Norbert Swaer, who at that time had fished on Green Bay for 55 years. The article does a good job of describing the life of a commercial fisherman but left out a lot of details, which Nancy has added. Norbert related in the article that he maneuvered the *Casey Bros.* away from the dock at 6 AM each morning, and fished every summer morning for perch in Green Bay. Then by noon, he would return with his catch, ready to transport it to market in the city of Green Bay. Norbert would return home around four each afternoon, and then he would repair his nets and ready his boat for the next morning.

In the article, Norbert recalled buying his first commercial fishing license back in 1939. He paid only $6 for the license, which at the time this article was written, cost him $750 per year.

Norbert also spoke about the quotas which had been placed on commercial fishermen. When fish were plentiful, Norbert said that he could switch between perch fishing and herring fishing in the Bay, but due to the quotas, he was reaching his annual limit by early September, making further fishing unprofitable. The herring has nearly disappeared from Green Bay (some Cisco Herring remain, and other than in Grand Traverse Bay, few are found on the Great Lakes anymore), and Norbert then fished for alewife in the late 60s and into the 70s, which was used for various purposes, other than human consumption. Perch fishing, using gill nets, was done from mid-summer into the fall.

However, Norbert did cite the fact that electronics had made it much easier to track fish, and it was also easier to find nets using GPS and autopilot, rather than searching by sight. Also, nylon netting has been a great improvement over the old cotton netting material.

Norbert said that he did not originally set out to become a fisherman. He was a third-generation fisherman, having fished with his father as a young boy. He went to Badger Business School after high school, and following graduation, he worked for a while as a billing clerk at a local cheese factory. After less than a year, he realized that he missed fishing and that a desk job did not suit him.

Norbert also stated that during his 55 years of commercial fishing, he had only missed two full years of fishing full-time, because he was delivering landing craft to the East Coast from local shipyards.

After working all of these years, Norbert and his wife, Margaret, enjoy traveling after his fishing quotas are met for the season. Norbert took up golf during their vacations in south Texas. He was still fishing in 1984 when that article was published, but only because he enjoyed it.

Norbert was still fishing whitefish in April 2004, but he entered the hospital in May of that same year. After several surgeries, he passed away in July. His wife, Margaret died in 2008, at age 89, and David died young, at age 62. Nancy and Dennis are doing well and were happy to help record their family's history.

SWAER FAMILY ICE FISHING

Most people think of ice fishing as being the guys sitting out on some frozen, inland lake, drinking beer and telling lies, waiting for the bell to sound on their "tip-up" next to a small hole they either chopped or augered into the ice. But on Green Bay (as well as other areas protected from winter winds on the Great Lakes), ice-fishing through the ice with gill nets was a necessary part of the commercial fishermen's lives, to survive the long winter, when they could not use boats for fishing.

We don't have a picture of Dennis Swaer while out ice fishing, but this is Dennis fishing shad (alewives) with his dad. Dennis was a wonderful resource for assembling this section of the book.

The following description of Commercial Ice Fishing was provided by Nancy Swaer's brother, Dennis Swaer., from when Dennis fished with his father, Norbert.

Nancy Swaer asked me if we wanted to include a section in this book, describing ice fishing. As a young boy, living on the shores of Green Bay, I witnessed commercial fishermen driving their old cars and trucks onto the Bay, and one winter I had a chance to accompany one of them, a friend of the family. I watched the process and learned enough to ask my parents if I could buy a couple small nets (50-footers) and set them like I had seen them being set during my excursion with those fishermen. I figured it out on my own and set and pulled those nets for two winters until high school brought other priorities into my life. We ate a lot of fish during those winters.

So, I was looking forward to getting the ice fishing section, which was written by Nancy's brother, Dennis Swaer. I didn't expect much, but as you will see below, Dennis did a "bang-up" job describing every part of the process. I cannot thank Dennis enough for all his work on this, including the great photos from his personal archives.

The following are Dennis's words:

INTRO TO COMMERCIAL ICE FISHING

My father, Norbert Swaer, was a dedicated commercial fisherman who, along with Margaret, his wife of over 60 years, raised a family on our river property in Pensaukee Wisconsin. Pensaukee is located on the west shore of Green Bay, about 25 miles north of the city of Green Bay. My parents had four children and in order of birth were named, Dennis, Carol, David, and Nancy.

We, kids, attended a one-room school with outdoor toilets (Wisconsin winters!), one teacher, and sometimes as many as fifty students. I was attending that grade school when I began helping Dad, and I continued through high school, college, and after returning from overseas duty in the Air

Force. Initially, my tasks were simple, but as I got older, they expanded to cover most aspects of the operation. That was many decades ago, and I am recalling these experiences as well as I can. I apologize in advance for any inaccuracies. Furthermore, the descriptions are related to my experiences starting in the 1950s and are not necessarily universal. That is to say that other fishermen may have used different equipment and done things differently.

Fishing was hard work and not always profitable. But families needed to be supported, not only during the open water season but also in winter. The Bay is about 120 miles long and 12 miles wide at Pensaukee. In winter, it freezes all the way across, with ice often a foot or thicker. Some fishermen did other work during the winter and some, like my father, put nets under the ice.

How does one travel over the Wisconsin ice and snow on a frozen body of water that often resembles the Arctic? How does one put nets under the ice? How does one get the fish out of the nets? What are some of the unique hazards created by this massive body of ice? What is it like out there?

EQUIPMENT

Left to right: Model A Ford, Rollie Breed, Herb Imig, and Norbert Swaer.

Model A Fords were often used in those days. They were simple, relatively lightweight, and had decent clearance. I learned to drive on that ice in one of those old four-bangers. Tire chains were usually used but weren't always sufficient.

In the 1950s and early 1960s, our snowmobile was a modified Model A Ford. An extra set of wheels, sometimes two sets, called "idlers," would be attached to the body in the center, and metal belts like tank tracks covered all four or six wheels. This provided great traction and limited sinking in deep snow. "Runners" replaced the front wheels. They were sometimes specially made and were sometimes fashioned out of old car bumpers welded to wheel rims, which were then attached where the front wheels would normally be. This version of a snowmobile could handle deep snow well but was not particularly responsive to turning. Often, repeated attempts were required over some distance to change direction. Some years later, machines looking more like the snowmobiles we see today began evolving.

Cold ride.

Less cold ride.

Another interesting modification to the Model A was the "boilerplate" approach. The same runners were used on the front, but instead of wheels with belts, large spiked discs of steel were mounted as rear wheels. The larger diameter steel wheels improved clearance and would slice through deep snow, and the spikes provided great traction.

The ride could be pretty bumpy, but I think it was more responsive to turning. There was at least one significant downside. If the vehicle did get stuck in the snow that covered the ice, spinning a wheel turned the boilerplate into a very effective ice saw. The reader can likely picture the result.

These vehicles sometimes had drilling machines mounted on them. Many holes were manually chopped in the ice with a heavy ice chisel, so these drills were a welcome piece of equipment. The drilling machine was attached to the front of the vehicle, and it was powered by a shaft that extended through the crank hole to the engine, located under the radiator. The business end of the drilling machine was a heavy metal disc that was attached to a vertical shaft in front of the vehicle. It could be raised or lowered, causing the disc to contact the ice in a flat plane like setting a pie pan on the ice. The disc had a pizza-like slice removed, and a sharp-toothed piece of metal attached on one side of the sliced opening. It angled slightly downward to extend a few inches below the disc. When powered up, the vertical shaft would turn the disc which was lowered onto the ice to begin chewing a hole. The size of the disc determined the size of the hole. (Much like the smaller augers used today by hobby fishermen.)

In addition to providing transportation and drilling holes, the model A sometimes towed a large sleigh and/or a lifting shanty. The sleigh carried boxes of nets and other tools and equipment used for setting the nets under the ice. Days later when the nets were lifted, the sleigh would hopefully carry boxes of fish.

The lifting shanty consisted of a wooden frame, resting on runners. The frame was covered with canvas, which on either end of the shanty was long enough to reach the ice but could be folded up enough to allow travel. These end curtains helped seal out the wind and cold when dropped, and then banked with snow. On the inside of the shanty, two cross pieces attached to the top side of each runner spanned the middle of the inside of the shanty. The cross pieces supported a stove that was often fashioned out of an old oil or gas drum. A board similarly mounted at either end of the inside served as a bench-type seat.

FROM THE FROZEN TUNDRA TO THE FROZEN BAY

As I lay in bed on a winter night, I would hear the eerie sound of the ice in the river and on the bay cracking as temperatures changed. I don't know how to describe the sound other than to say, to me, it sounded like a gun, sometimes a very large gun, being fired underwater.

The contracting ice created hazards when traveling on the Bay, especially in the early morning hours when the ice surface was coldest and the cracks opened. Cracks running roughly parallel to the shore and at various distances further out, would open up from a few inches to several feet, and sometimes wide enough to swallow a vehicle.

In the morning after breakfast, we would bundle up, put on felt shoes inside our rubber boots, grab our lunch buckets, and climb into the frigid cab of an old Model A Ford. Starting the engine involved twisting the ignition wires together (the key was long gone), setting both the spark advance/retard lever and the throttle on the steering column, adjusting the choke lever, which was a rod on the passenger side, connected directly to the carburetor, and then stepping on the starter, which was somewhere on the floorboard on the driver side. I vividly recall the sound of the starter cranking the engine, the sound the engine made when it first started, and then how it changed in tone as the ignition lever was adjusted from starting position to the running position.

So, while this contortionist engine starting event took place, our breathing added to the frost already on the windshield. There was no heater/defroster comparable to what we have in today's vehicles. Instead, a system similar to, but not even as good as, the old Volkswagen bug would eventually provide some heat. Dad would scrape a little hole in the frost on the windshield to look through while his tobacco smoke added to the reduced visibility. I sometimes just rode blind for a while, more focused on trying to stay warm.

Because we lived on the west shore, we would be driving east into the sun in the morning making it more difficult to spot a new crack. The older cracks were usually easier to discern in good weather because the ice had shoved and buckled during the warm part of previous days, creating what looked like mini-mountain ranges. And due to the lack of features, other than snow-covered ice for perspective, it was sometimes difficult to ascertain the distance and size of these features. Drifting snow created an added challenge. And the more recent cracks were less likely to have ice cakes piled up, making them harder to spot.

It was important to be able to stop and assess a crack. If it was not too wide, Dad might say, "Ok son, hang on, we're going to jump the crack." I found this exciting because it involved starting some distance back and gunning the engine to build up enough speed so that the wheels would skip over the crack without dropping in. When it was determined too hazardous to "jump the crack", we would use planks we called bridges. They needed to be placed in such a way, that when spanning the crack, the boards didn't move when driven over. I usually didn't get to ride in the vehicle when it was driven on those bridges.

Dad told a story about a crack crossing that didn't go so well. As I recall the story, his brother Clarence "Ike" was driving into the sun one morning on glare ice, in a Model "T" Ford. When he realized he was approaching a wide-open crack and wouldn't be able to stop, he went to full throttle hoping to "jump the crack." The front wheels made it across but both tires blew and the starting crank wrapped down and under the radiator. The rear wheels fared worse. They hit with enough force to detach the rear axle, which dropped into the bay, while the rest of the vehicle skidded forward on the front wheels and rear part of the body.

SETTING GILLNETS UNDER THE ICE

How does one put nets under the ice? The gillnets we set were each 200 feet long. A box of nets was usually five nets and a "gang" of nets consisted of several boxes of nets all connected end to end. So, a gang could range in length from 1000 feet to a mile or more.

After deciding on a place to set the nets, we would chop a hole with an ice chisel or drill a hole in the ice with the drilling machine. Then a 100-foot-long "running pole" consisting of boards slightly overlapped at their ends and nailed together, would be fed into the hole in the desired direction. Once the entire length of wood was in the water and floating up against the undersurface of the ice, a piece of light line over 200 feet long would be attached. The next step was to go 100 feet from the hole and hopefully locate the far end of the running pole which was easy when there was minimal snow and clear ice. If the ice was unclear and/or covered with significant snow, we would need to pace off or measure 100 ft and search. Another hole would be made at that point and a "running pole hook" was used to work the running pole another 100 feet along its way, under the ice. Again, we would locate the end and make a third hole and again use the running pole hook, to push the pole another 100 feet. At this point, there would be 200 feet of running line under the ice, extending from the first hole to the third hole.

The running line would then be detached from the running pole and tied to the end of a net. A major part of my job when I was a youngster, was to pick up the opposite end of the running line, sling it over my shoulder, and begin walking. This would pull the net that Dad was tending into the water and under the ice. I recall it would go pretty easy at first, but as more netting was fed into the water, creating drag, it would become more challenging, especially on bare ice. We typically wore "creepers", which were small metal pieces with four tines, that fit under the instep of our boots for better traction. After one net was completely under the ice, it was tied off at both ends to an upright stick in the ice that both served to mark the location of the hole and help hold the net in place. This process was repeated until the desired number of nets was set.

"LIFTING" THE NETS

![truck on ice]

In later years we traveled in greater comfort when conditions permitted.

After a day or two, sometimes more, we would return to "lift" the nets. The holes were located and reopened, and the lifting shanty was pulled into place over one of the holes. End curtains were dropped and snow, if available, was banked against the curtains and runners. A fire would be started in the stove and the running line attached to the far end of a net, 200 feet from the shanty. It would feed into the water and under the ice as the net was pulled by hand into the shanty.

My brother David attaching the running line to the net

A gillnet, when in the water, is like a meshed fence setting on or near the Bay's bottom. Mesh size is tailored to the species being fished and is strictly regulated. The top rail, or "float line," has floatation attached every ten feet. In the early days, these "floats" were made of wood and then varnished, to keep them from becoming waterlogged. They were replaced by aluminum floats, as can be seen neatly stacked in the following picture. I have also seen plastic floats. The lead line was strung with weights every ten feet, opposite the floats, and they would sink, forming the bottom of the "fence." The weights were made by pouring hot molten lead into molds.

I can recall that we mostly fished for perch, whitefish, and herring, although several other species were caught in smaller quantities and sold. After the entire net was in the lifting shanty, and the fish removed, the net was pulled back under the ice with the running line.

My brother David pulling the running line and the net back into the water under the ice.

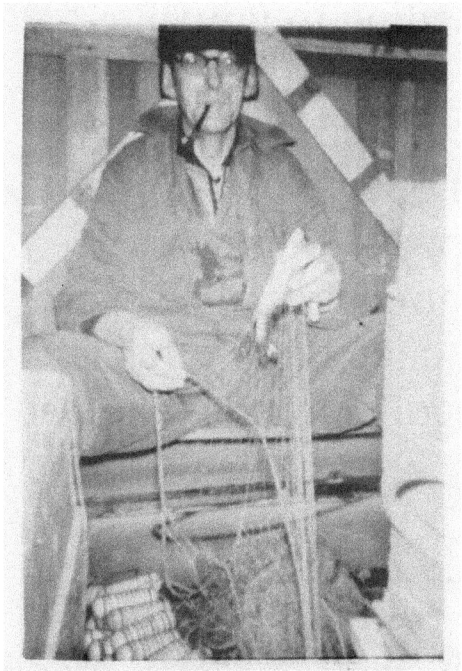

Norbert Swaer lifting perch nets in winter. Notice the bare hands. That water is cold.

I enjoyed eating lunch in the lifting shanty. We often toasted our sandwiches on the stove. Then, as the day warmed, the sound of the ice responding to the temperature change was like distant thunder. Sometimes the pressure of the ice expanding would build until something had to give. The "give" often resulted in a crack where the ice would buckle and pile up. To my way of thinking, it was like a small earthquake. The noise was an impressive rumble, and the motion would slosh the water in the open holes.

Whitefish being readied for the trip back to Pensaukee

Ice can move in unexpected ways, leading to unwanted consequences. One year, I recall that the ice, where Dad had set nets, broke loose and became a free-floating ice field. There would have to have been open water some distance out in the Bay for this to happen. Nets were precious. A pilot, named Jubin, was hired to make several trips with a small plane, to land on the ice field to retrieve the nets and probably the fish. My recollection is that Dad lost a lifting shanty, but no vehicles.

AL STRANZ COMMENTED ON DENNIS'S STORY ABOVE:

"The pilot that landed on the ice was probably Bob Jubin. He ran the Oconto airport for many years. He had been a P47 pilot in WW II. He was a real character."

THE POWER OF ICE

Another year, as the ice was breaking up but still very thick, a strong wind pushed the ice toward and onto the west shore. My uncle, Art Swaer, had a nice cottage on the Bay at Oak Orchard. The ice slowly and relentlessly pushed onto the shore, through the east wall of the cottage, and into the house. The living room was filled with thick ice cakes. Ice moving in this manner also created large piles of ice in the Bay, when it encountered resistance from the Bay's bottom, in areas of shallower water.

ICE FOLLIES

My brother, Dave, unwittingly discovered another hidden danger. The Bay had frozen out quite a distance from the shore, but not all the way across. At some point, an ice field broke free and drifted away. As the freezing continued, the ice that did not break away continued to freeze thick enough to easily support a vehicle. The area beyond that thicker ice had become open water but froze over again. Because it was a more recent freeze, it was not as thick. Mother Nature added another twist by dropping a light snow.

My brother and a friend decided to drive on the Bay a couple miles from Pensaukee, to a resort up the shore at Oak Orchard (Johnson's I think) to get cigarettes and or beer. The trip went well until his Chevy encountered the transition from the older, thicker ice, onto the newer, thinner ice. He and his friend climbed out the windows as the car was sinking and managed to get on the ice and walk home.

We went out the next day and discovered we could see the roof of the car a couple feet below the surface. Dad, accustomed to improvising, hatched a plan to retrieve Dave's car. We went to shore and then returned to the sunken car with a block and tackle, a post, the wood plank bridges described earlier, some chain, and a long pole with a hook on the end. The bridges were slid down behind and in line with the rear wheels, spanning from the

Bay bottom to the surface of the ice. The pole was employed, with some difficulty, to loop the chain over the trailer hitch at the back of the car. The post was anchored in the ice and served as a "dead head" for the block and tackle. Dad's truck pulled the block and tackle rope, which was attached to the chain, and the car began to move backward up the bridges, more easily at first because it was submerged. The process was slowed down to let water drain as the car rose above the surface. Eventually, the car was towed to Pensaukee and into a heated shanty. The result was that the car was restored to a road-worthy condition, though some water remained and saturated the upholstery.

My brother was a drummer in a band at that time, and he got a call from a member who usually pulled the band trailer. His car had broken down and he knew Dave had a trailer hitch on his car, so he asked Dave to drive the band trailer. It was a cold winter night and the car was parked outside as usual, but it ran pretty well and the heater worked. After picking up a couple band members and their girlfriends, he heard one of the girls complain that the back seat was really hard. Dave said to just wait a little while and it would soften up. Of course, that created a new issue.

CONCLUSION

A frozen bay presents unique circumstances. Commercial ice fishing is hard work, with challenges both obvious and hidden. The conditions in Green Bay can be brutal when the temperatures are near zero Fahrenheit, the wind is blowing, and the snow is drifting, stinging the face, and making the way home difficult to find. There are also sunny days with little or no wind when it was warm enough to go without a jacket. I remember stepping out of the lifting shanty and painfully squinting into the blinding whiteness. I also recall the great satisfaction of coming home with the day's catch.

This was a unique way to grow up and learn about nature, work, and play. I consider myself fortunate to have had these experiences.

PENSAUKEE, WISCONSIN

Nancy Swaer supplied the following history of Pensaukee, where the Swaer family and others fished for many years. Pensaukee has only one remaining commercial fisherman.

Pensaukee was a booming fishing village when Nancy was growing up there. It also had a rich history of commercial fishing well before her time. Several families/neighbors and relatives lived and fished out of Pensaukee. Some names she recalled were Livermore, Imig, Topel,

Breed, Kulpa, and Brunette, but there were many more before that of which Nancy wouldn't know.

Pensaukee also had a lumber mill across the river from Nancy's family home, in earlier times. The slip on the Swaer property, where Nancy's dad docked the Casey Bros. was once where logs were floated in and pulled to shore for transporting. There was a general store in the center of the village, which was two properties away from the Swaer's house.

Pensaukee also had a three-story (plus the basement, making four) hotel.

The Gardner House was described as the most elegant and largest hotel north of Milwaukee. It was built in 1872 but was destroyed by a tornado five years later in 1877. The general store was later built on the foundation of the hotel.

THE GARDNER HOUSE WAS THE BEST IN THE NORTH

FIRST CATCH

I was almost ready to send the manuscript for this book to my designer when I received a referral from a friend, another marine surveyor. He said that he was contacted by a fisherman out of L'Anse, Michigan, who was buying an older fish tug from another fisherman in Door County. That fisherman called me, and we arranged a time to meet at the boat in question, to inspect the boat for his lender. That man is Paul Smith, and the name of his company is **FIRST CATCH**.

I told Paul about the book I was putting together and asked him if he would be interested in giving me some stories to be included in the book. What follows are Paul's stories about his family, and how they became involved in commercial fishing.

This first picture is of the "Norska," which Paul will use for fishing out of L'Anse. The Norska was on dry land during our inspection, with not enough open space to take a clear overall picture. So, this photo was provided by Chris Petersen.

Unlike most stories in this book, I would say mine is a creation story. The original, the first. I don't have a family line of fishermen with knowledge passed down to me from generation to generation. However, I like to say that fishing is in my blood, even though I come from a family of law enforcement. I still heard the "calling of the sea."

My story begins when I was in my youth. My older sister was part of my tribe's hatchery program. She was one of the three people that started the program. I remember taking part in planting lake trout in the Keweenaw Bay area, and all the steps involved from spawning the fish to incubation to rearing, and then eventually planting. As the tribe's hatchery program grew, youth programs began to support efforts to have summer interns, which I fully took part in.

I remember one instance when I was about 16 years old, we just finished doing assessments on the lake. After the quantity of fish was recorded and we finished for the day, the tribal biologist at the time asked me if I wanted the fish. I replied, "sure." Not fully understanding what he meant by "taking some fish", I helped myself to about 400lbs. I loaded up and went to the local icehouse to get more ice for the fish. I then stopped for gas, and as I was filling up, someone next to me noticed all the fish I had.

He asked if he could have some, and I said it wasn't a problem. The gentleman went to the back of his truck and retrieved a cooler, brought it over, and took about 10 lake trout and 5 jumbo white fish. He brought the cooler back to his truck, which I thought was the end of the transaction. What happened next surprised me. He returned and handed me a twenty-dollar bill. I asked what it was for, and he told me it was for the fish and called me silly. I remember looking at the unexpected money in my hand with a little bit of shock, then I looked at the remaining fish in my truck.

That's when it hit me like a ton of bricks. I had an "ah-ha" moment. It was the first time I looked at boxes of fish and didn't see fish…I saw money. Needless to say, I spent the rest of the afternoon peddling fish around the reservation. Before any of our readers judge me, remember I was a 16-year-old kid; and the $20 I got at the gas station was enough to fill up my truck, and I still had about 350 lbs. of "gas money" in my possession.

Later that evening, when I returned home, my sister came over to my mom's house and asked me what I did with all the fish. I told her, "I went around the reservation asking for 'donations'." As you can imagine, she wasn't too happy with me. She and my mother had me go back to the people I peddled the fish to and offer them their money back. Lucky for me, none of them wanted it back. Completely unaware, my first experience with fishing was with black market fish. In a way, I have been chasing that first "ah-ha" high my entire life.

I recall some of the fishing tugboat owners in my area, one owner in particular. His name was Gerry Jondreau. He was the owner of the "Boyzie II," named after his father, William Boyzie Jondreau, who battled the State of Michigan over the fishing rights for tribal people and won. At that time, Gerry was retired, but he still loved to fish. When I was about 16 or 17, Gerry had an operation and lost a foot, so he hired me to assist him with his boat. As he prepared throughout that winter to do some fishing, I would spend time learning as much as I could, listening to his stories, and doing odd jobs.

Unfortunately, one day when we went to do some maintenance on his boat, someone had broken into his tug and opened the water valves, sinking his boat at the dock. I remember Gerry having a ghostly look on his face. However, despite all of that, he looked at me and asked, "Paul, do you see what I see?" I replied, "A sunken tugboat." He said, "Look closer." Well, I didn't get it at first, but the exhaust stack was still above the surface. Gerry explained, "As long as the exhaust stack stays above the surface, the engine will not flood."

Again, not fully understanding the complexities of what the tribal fisheries had endured at this point, I asked myself, why? Why would someone want to sink a fishing boat? Later that summer, another boat was broken into, and it too was sunk at the dock. I remember the day Gerry had his boat lifted out of the water and pumped, and I also remember the day Gerry had started up the boat after pulling it out of the water; I had to carry that heavy 24-volt battery. We swapped out the batteries and within the first or second attempt, the engine turned over. Gerry, with a facial expression of full determination, looked over at me and said, "What did I tell ya?"

Gerry had moved his boat around from port to port, and of course, I was always up for the boat ride. He got that boat back into working order, but never set another gill net. I remember the last voyage of the "Boyzie II". Gerry, my brother Steve, and I left South Entry in the middle of December and traveled to the Baraga Marina. The trip was less than pleasant. He intended to dock the boat at the marina for the winter However, the elderly woman who owned the bait store nearby expressed her opinion about the "eye sore" of a boat belonging at the bottom of the lake, so Gerry decided to move the "Boyzie II" to the Pequaming Marina. There it sat and faded with time after Gerry's passing.

Remember when I mentioned I come from a family line of law enforcement? Well, my tribe was expanding its conservation enforcement and hired several officers; I was one of them. The tribe developed the concept of a "Home Territory" to establish a claim to certain waters and lands within the 1842 Treaty area. It was up to the Keweenaw

Bay Indian Community to manage the natural resources and enforce the laws that the tribe established. I spent the next few years doing what I could to help the local tribal commercial fishermen. I remember one fisherman had engine problems and needed help getting his net out of the water. I was recently back from basic training at the Indian Police Academy. Eager to help, I jumped in the hatchery boat to go to help him. This wasn't the best decision I had ever made. The hatchery boat was a 20-ft. open bow, and it was December. Very cold.

During my first shot at law enforcement, I was involved for about 4 years, and after attempting employment in three different police departments, I decided to make my way back home to my reservation. By this time in my life, I was married, then divorced, and had my two boys, Dasan and Talon (seen in this picture as youngsters).

Looking for an income, I decided to go to college and take advantage of the educational benefits the tribe had to offer. While doing so, I had the bright idea to start commercial fishing.

One of the people who helped my sister start the tribe's hatchery was a technician named Neil. Neil had quit that job to fish full-time. He had two tugboats at that time, one he called the "Katherine," named after his now ex-wife, and another he bought from Thill's Fish Market in Marquette, MI. I don't recall the name of that tug.

After deciding to become a commercial fisherman, I sat down with Neil at his home and told him my plan. I believe the reason he was so accepting of me and willing to share his trade secrets had something to do with an interaction I had with him and his wife in the winter of 2004-05. The bay was frozen over, and I was patrolling the area with my partner, Mo. It was easy enough in the wintertime to spot the fishermen. All you had to do was scan the sky for a flock of seagulls, or the ice for blood from the fish. Mo and I came to a location in front of the "Mission Church,' or the village of Assinins. We could see two people pulling up a net through the ice, with the seagulls circling above and blood on the ice. Mo and I looked at each other, "Too easy, let's go check them out." We walked out on the ice to find Neil and his wife at the time, Katherine/Kathy.

Our tribal law states, if you are a big boat commercial fisherman, you cannot set gillnets in the "on-reservation" waters. Having two tugboats, Neil was considered a big boat fisherman, and we were surely on reservation waters. Neil, being the sly guy that he is, explained that he was not fishing, he was helping his wife pull a subsistence net. Our tribal law also states that if you're a commercial fisherman you cannot set a subsistence net. Being that

Kathy had her subsistence license and it was currently valid, all was good. However, while we were talking with Neil and his wife, and observing what they were doing, the local fish market owner, Brad, walked up, pulling 4 empty fish boxes on a sled. I asked Brad what he was up to, not in an official enforcement capacity, but sincerely curious as to the reason he was pulling a sled full of empty fish boxes out on the ice. Of course, Brad said something to the effect that he was heading to his ice shanty.

About an hour later, Mo and I were traveling on the highway, and we saw Brad's truck parked outside his fish house/market. Mo and I looked at each other and had a "no way… they didn't" moment. So, we stopped and talked to Brad. Brad was very persistent that the fish he was processing was his fish. Without having a straight-up confession that he bought the fish from Neil and his wife, or Neil saying he sold the fish to Brad, we had the strongest circumstantial case ever. Over the next few days, Mo and I did some digging around, we spoke to Neil again, and he didn't tell us much more, "What you see is what you get," was his policy on speaking to law enforcement. When we spoke to our tribal prosecutor at that time, she asked, "Did you touch the fish, how could you tell it was fresh, were there any unique identifying factors to the fish?" …etc. Unknown to us at that time, the tribal prosecutor was very determined to see this case through to the end.

Later in the week, Mo and I acquired some fish. Later at the office, for lunch, we decided to cook it up on the grill. It was something that we were known to do. Just as we were finished cooking the fish, the tribal prosecutor came into the office and complimented us, "That smells good." We began to strike up a conversation with her and towards the end, she brought up the case about Neil,

"So, where are you with that case with the fisherman?" she asked. Mo replied, "It's over, closed, done with," The prosecutor, with a confused look on her face, asked, "Why? I thought you caught him red-handed." Mo replied with a grin on his face, "Well, you're eating the evidence."

At that time, the tribal police department had its office at the tribal center, the main government office for the tribe. News of what happened didn't take long to make its way through the tribal center. Of course, the prosecutor wasn't really eating the evidence, but the joke spread too quickly for us to do any damage control.

My mother, who raised me, was the local Bureau of Indian Affairs law enforcement officer. She did a mixture of police and conservation enforcement. She was very by the book, giving little to no breaks. As we are located on the Keweenaw Bay Indian Community reservation, consequently she was given the nickname, "The Bitch of the Bay." Now, did Mo and I see the transaction of the fish sale between Neil and Brad? No. Did Mo and I push it any further? No, we didn't. So, when I spoke to Neil about becoming a fisherman later on, he brought up the fact that he felt that, as a conservation officer, I was fair and didn't make things up to strengthen an accusation. I guess that is how I earned enough of his respect for him to teach me the ins and outs of the business.

That summer, Neil took me under his wing, bringing me out on the water in his tug, and on the little 16-foot boat that he sold me to start with. Whenever I would face any of the challenges associated with commercial fishing, he was always quick to say, with laughter, "So, you wanna be a fisherman, hey?" Always bringing up the complexities of my current struggle.

I remember a trip where Neil and I went to go retrieve our nets. I was still in Neil's "training phase." We went to my net first and the result was less than satisfying. I ended up with 200-300 lbs. of suckers and carp. As we got closer to Neil's net, I was shocked at what I saw. It was so full of fish that it was floating on the surface. Of course, taking the opportunity to rub it in, Neil was quick to say, "That's how you fish!" He had fished in the area where I had my net, so he knew that area would be loaded with suckers and carp. Instead of advising me to set elsewhere, he wanted me to experience prospecting or getting to know the lake. ~ Point taken, my friend. ~

Here is a picture of the boat Neil sold me. I found this picture on the internet, and those are the two fishermen I sold the boat to. Unfortunately, without my permission, they continue to operate a fishing business under my pseudonym, "First Catch." I didn't know it at the time, or I would have said something. Karma is a funny thing, though.

Around that time there was a federal sting operation that got a lot of black-market sales identified, and that's all I am going to say about that. I don't hold a grudge against these two. Simply put, I don't think they knew any better. Even though I sold them the boat, I noticed they needed some fishing equipment, so I guess I permanently loaned them my fish boxes. They must have needed it more than I did at that time.

I remember that boat having a standard bow, with rowboat-style seating. My brother Joe and I put a piece of treated wood over it to make a platform for pulling nets.

Though I started out fishing with Neil, after a while, it was time to let go and do it myself. That's when the real challenges began: long hours, back-breaking work, chasing after fish sales, and competing with the other local tribal fishermen; it was a cutthroat business. The restaurants around here knew it, and they fed into that. Fishermen were dropping prices on their fish just to make a sale. No one ever told me, that part of commercial fishing, you're going to have to understand a lot more about the business end than you do the fishing part of it.

I realized I needed help. For my second season, I reached out to my brother Joe. It didn't take much convincing. I said to him, "You wanna fish with me? I don't know how it's going to go, but we can split everything evenly… ⅓ to you, ⅓ to me, and ⅓ back to the business." Joe's response was, "Let's do it." As you can see in this picture, Joe is standing on the platform we built for the first boat I owned.

We were catching fish, and, of course, we were happy about it. We started small … really small. I think when this picture was taken, I was fishing with only 1,200 feet (about 365.76 m) of gill net, as was Joe. We would mainly be in the Keweenaw Bay area, "on-reservation" as our laws called it.

The bay protected smaller operations from a lot of winds and weather. If the wind was blowing from the west, you would simply make your way to the west of the bay to be protected by the land. The same concept was used for the easterly winds, on the rare occasions they would appear. It was always the southwest wind that would shut down the bay. If you got caught up in that, it would blow you right out of the bay. At times, Joe and I had that boat packed so full of fish and gear that there couldn't have been more than 4 inches of clearance before the boat started to get swamped out by waves coming over the sides.

As you can see by the map, the red line illustrates the reservation for the Keweenaw Bay Indian Community. Joe and I spent a lot of time prospecting around the bay.

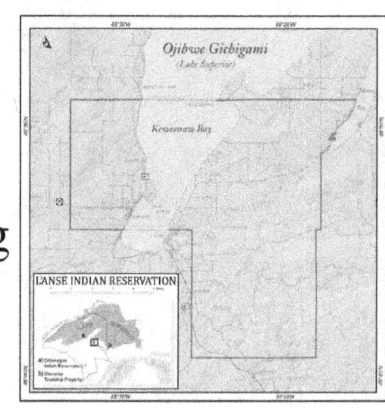

Our father, Dave, grew up on the eastern shoreline of the bay, in a house the family still affectionately refers to as "the blue house." Our grandfather, a non-Indian, Finnish fisherman, would set gill nets in the bay to support his family. That is until restrictions against gill-net fishing for non-Indian fishermen were imposed. That was when our father told us that he had to continue fishing as a teen, being that he was native. He is now retired from the Department of Natural Resources for the State of Michigan as a conservation officer. As I said before, I come from a line of law enforcement. But, if anything was contributing to the calling of the sea, I think it's safe to say, it came from his side.

To the left is a picture of me and my cousins, Laurie and Liz. Three grandchildren, from three different children, who were raised by my father's father. Here we are, cleaning fish at the Baraga Village Marina's fish cleaning station.

Laurie and Liz had been bugging me about going out on the lake to fish. They wanted to go with me while I pulled my nets, so they could enjoy the bounty as well. Instead, I let Laurie borrow one of my nets and challenged them to do their own subsistence fishing with me. Most of the family who heard this did not think Liz could handle it, but she was determined.

So, with my dad's boat at the time, I took them out to retrieve the subsistence net I had let Laurie borrow. Of course, since I had the extra help on board, I went to retrieve my own net, which happened to be twice as long as Laurie's. If they wanted fish, they were going to earn it! That day, we ended up with a lot of fish to clean.

Surprisingly enough, the girls handled it fine, and have continued to return to the lake when they can. They went as far as purchasing their own net from my supplier, so they could continue their efforts when they have the opportunity.

A funny story came to mind while digging for these pictures. When Joe and I would come off the lake, we would bring our catch to the cleaning station located at the Baraga Village Marina. We would spend about an hour or more cleaning our fish. It wasn't a sophisticated set-up, just a little bit of shelter and a water supply to keep the fish clean and rinsed. We would always leave the cleaning station in better shape than we had found it. We figured we were helping by cleaning it while using the facility.

One day, we came to the cleaning station, and on one of the posts was a sign that read, "Sport Fishermen Only." I remember feeling so insulted. I didn't understand why the village staff didn't come speak to me directly if there was a problem.

Well, I unloaded my fish and began to clean it anyway. It wasn't long before the person who owned the bait shop came up to me and asked if I could read. I said, "I can read fine. What do you need help with?" Well, of course, he wasn't too happy with my response. He instructed me to leave the area and said that I was causing damage to the cleaning station. I asked him if he could explain. Well, our tribal laws require us to put plastic tags on each clean lake trout. This happens after the fish is harvested. Our laws don't mention the processing of fish, so we left the tags with the remains.

One of the tribal police supervisors came down to the marina and repeated what the bait shop owner had told me. I reminded them both that I was in a public place on the reservation, and that I was not the one causing a disturbance. The bait shop owner finally admitted that what we were doing didn't harm any of the equipment, but rather that our tags were creating a clog in the pipes, which the village staff had to address a couple of times. The clog wasn't even happening in the equipment near the cleaning station, but further down the system, after the bait shop. Later on, my brother and I just changed our fishing schedule and then cut the tags before discarding the remains of the fish. I guess in the end, what they don't know won't hurt them.

As time passed, my boys found their way out on the water. During this time, my brother would spend the week with me and my boys in my HUD house on the reservation. On the weekends we would head to my brother's place in Ishpeming. Times were tough. The fish we didn't sell each day, we ended up cooking to eat for ourselves. My boys were eventually so sick of fish, I had

to come up with new ways to feed it to them. So, "chicken fish" was invented. It was cooked the same way and it tasted the same, but if you asked me about it, I'd tell you it was different. That lasted for a while until my boys requested fish and chicken fish at the same time. The jig was up. I still occasionally offer up a satisfying meal of chicken fish to this day.

Eventually, just like I did, my boys started looking at fish as money. They would try and keep track of the number of fish I caught and try to figure out how many boxes of fish would equal a new game system. I marked that up as a proud moment. When my boys were in elementary school, I remember my oldest, Dasan, making deals with his friends' dads for fish. When I asked him about it, he told me they were bartering. Another proud moment.

Over the years, the boys wanted to be included in as much fishing as possible, either with the gillnets or with spearfishing. So, I believe in their minds, they owned just as much of the catch as I did. Their mother, my ex-wife, is of Native American descent like me, but she didn't grow up on the reservation. The term we used is "City Indian." Well, one spring, the boys and I had a great harvest of walleye that we stored in a freezer on our porch. Later in the year, they were having a family reunion on their mother's side.

I remember asking them the details of the event because sharing parenting time seems to be a never-ending battle. They told me it was going to be at their aunt's house, who lives in the same town as I do. Little did I know, the boys were conned into supplying the fish for this reunion. I remember coming home, looking in my freezer, and finding it completely empty. I knew I had some inventory left over, and, as a matter of fact, I knew I had a lot left over, but not anymore. It was all gone. I started blaming the usual suspects; my nephews and my cousins. Later, I found out that Dasan had gotten a ride to my house from his mother, and initiated operation "frozen walleye," taking all the walleye I had at the time. When I asked Dasan about the fish, the only thing he had to say was that "it was good." The disappointing part about the situation was that I didn't get any of it. Sure, I might have been a little upset in the beginning, but I eventually saw things from Dasan's point of view. Even though the fish he took came from my freezer, Dasan knew those were his fish, too.

When I decided to contribute to this book, my first thought was to talk to my sister, Catherine, for some ideas. She has always been my sounding board for all things fishing, even though she has never technically been on a boat with me. Catherine is one of my biggest supporters, backing me in whatever way she can, whether it be cosigning a loan (or two, or three), or simply giving words of encouragement when everyone else seemed to have nothing but doubt about my plans. I called Catherine to ask her what came to mind when she thinks about my fishing endeavors. She laughed. Her phone had just blasted the sound of a foghorn, the ringtone she had carefully selected for me. She told me that she thinks of the struggles I've had to overcome with regulations on my food trailer, battling the stigma of black-market fish sales, and the fact that I have done my best to include everyone when running this family business. I am beyond grateful for the support and contributions from my entire family, particularly Catherine and her husband, Mark.

My other sister, Evelyn, was the one who worked for the tribe's natural resources department. If it was anyone's fault for showing me the concepts of commercial fishing at a young age, the blame rests with her. Though she wasn't a commercial fisher herself, doing assessments and fish data collection was what planted the seed for me with commercial fishing, I think. Evelyn supports me in her own way, some may say she and I are on opposite sides of the battlefield when it comes to fishing, but I still think it's great to have that understanding of the bigger picture, getting a view from both perspectives. I remember one fishing trip, Evelyn and my mother were very worried about me fishing beyond the protection of the bay. They were adamant that I go with someone. I think this was one of the times my brother Joe had something else going on for that week and was unable to fish. So, Evelyn decided to help. Well, I think my entire family would agree that if I didn't have bad luck, I wouldn't have any luck at all.

By this time, I had replaced my engine as the motor head cracked on my first outboard. The replacement engine didn't last long. Evelyn and I had pulled up to the first string of nets. While I started pulling the net, she helped by gutting and icing the fish. Once we were done, it was time to reset. The wind was starting to pick up and the waves were getting bigger. I attempted to pull-start the engine. Nothing. Again and again, I tried to start the engine. Nothing was happening, and my sister wasn't too impressed with what was happening.

So, I decided to do some on-the-spot fixes. This required pulling the engine off the back and taking off the lanyard. I made my adjustments and put the engine back on. Well, I forgot to reattach the lanyard. While I was fixing the engine, somehow the throttle got turned up. As I pulled the cord to start the engine, it revved up. Naturally, I throttled down and put the engine in reverse to begin setting the net. Apparently, I didn't screw down the clamps holding the engine to the boat tight enough. With the waves rocking the boat up and down, and because I was going in reverse, the outboard locked itself in an upward position, as it would be if I was trailering it down the road. It then began pulling itself up off the back of the boat. I still had my hand on the throttle, but the way the engine lifted off the back of the boat, it fell into the water, causing the throttle to idle up.

I didn't want to let go. Picture this, my new (to me) 25-HP outboard, "free dancing" behind my boat, like something you would see in a cartoon, with me still holding on, trying not to let go. My sister looked on in shock, not believing what she was witnessing. The engine eventually went under and stalled. I looked at it, as it was suspended a few feet behind the boat, with the fuel line still attached. I started to pull on the line, just hoping that it wouldn't give way. I guess that was too much to ask for. It broke from the fuel disconnect and I watched as it disappeared into the water. The paddle to shore wasn't fun, but we made it back. I'm pretty sure that was the last time I think my sister was ever on the water...at least with me.

However, Evelyn's kids all pitched in with fishing in some way or another. Some were eager, while others were more reluctant to get involved. Evelyn's boys enjoyed being on the water and were happy to help. Evelyn's daughter, Katrina, not so much. I remember a time when Katrina and I were on the water, I had just finished pulling a net. As you can imagine, the area was swarming with seagulls. Katrina wanted to protect herself and was insisting she gets something to put on to avoid the seagull droppings. Being the clever uncle that I am, I poked three holes into a garbage bag and handed it to her. Less than pleased by the conditions of her work environment, Katrina gave me the most intense death glare, as she put on a black sticky garbage bag to gut fish. Even though Katrina didn't enjoy the water, she did have a huge part in the business when I went from fishing and peddling to buying my food trailer and selling my own fish.

I purchased the food trailer in the spring of 2019. The idea was to break away from the cut-throat business of trying to undercut prices to make a sale.

The other fishermen in the area had their established methods and routines. By this time, I had been away from fishing for a while. I knew I had to do something different if I wanted to get back in the game. I had made a couple of attempts to sell fish to some local establishments, but all were "loyal" to whoever was selling them fish at that time. Motivated to press on, I finished the purchase of the trailer. This was the beginning of one of the biggest struggles I had to endure in my business. Not because it wasn't a good idea, but because of the unforeseen politics and regulations it sparked in the area. The idea with the food trailer was to travel to events and bring my product to the community.

For our very first event, Katrina and I, along with my family, traveled to a powwow in Lower Michigan. As expected, we had to have a local health inspection. During the inspection, we were asked questions about the source of the fish, how long I have been fishing, where the fish gets cleaned, how the fish is caught, etc. After answering all the questions, I received his approval. Unfortunately, it was a small powwow and the turnout wasn't what we were hoping for.

We returned home, setting our sights on our next event, the Lake Trout Festival. That didn't turn out the way I was hoping, either. In my particular situation, I am licensed to fish through the Keweenaw Bay Indian Community. Therefore, I don't have to follow the regulations set forth by the state. So, in my mind, since I was operating my business in the treaty area of my tribe, I didn't need to ask the state for permission to sell my fish, like I did when I went to Lower Michigan. The problem became, I am a tribal fisherman who is regulated by the Bureau of Indian Affairs for public safety, by the tribe, for my fishing activities, and I was operating a food trailer in my ceded territory without the state's permission.

Before this, when I would go fishing, the state could not regulate how I was fishing. I could take that fish and go sell it to whoever I wanted, on or off the reservation. Now that I wanted to do this with my food trailer, and add value to my product, the state wanted to regulate the activity. This quickly became a problem. Even though the health department for the state was creating friction for my operation at this point, it was something that identified some concerns that the tribe wanted to address.

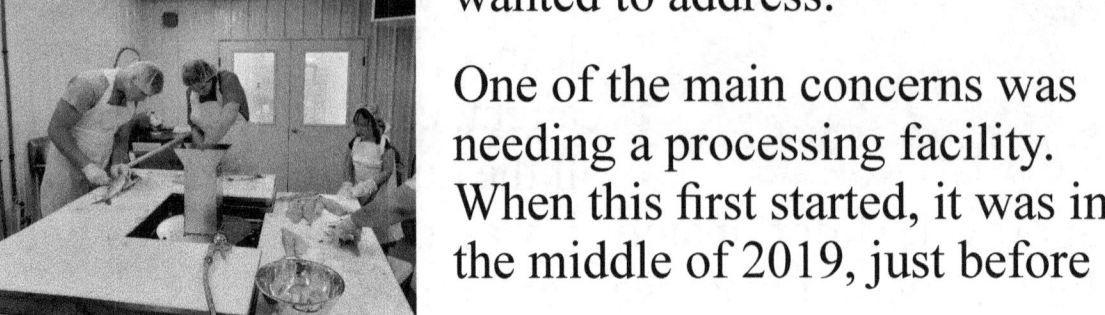

One of the main concerns was needing a processing facility. When this first started, it was in the middle of 2019, just before

Covid broke out. The fish processing facility was not finished until 2022. When it was finally complete, my operation was the first to use it, and the facility was the first to be recognized by the state as an approved facility for our tribe. What did this mean? Going and selling fish off the reservation in my food trailer wasn't a big deal to the state anymore.

Between 2019 and 2022, I had to process the fish in my food trailer. This created a problem as I wasn't open as much as I would have liked. Even with the extra help of my boys fishing with me, and Katrina running the food trailer, I couldn't keep the trailer stocked with enough fish. I was always running out. This was while we were only doing local events in the community and being parked at the tribe's local RV park. I had to figure out how to increase production, so, I was gonna need a bigger boat. I decided to look for the biggest boat I could find, while still maintaining my status as a small boat fisherman. This is where I found the "Angela Monique."

You know that whole "If I didn't have bad luck, I wouldn't have any luck," thing? The name "Angela Monique" represented something very different to me than it did for the previous owner (just ask my ex-wife).

So much so, I decided to go against superstition and rename the boat the "Wynonna Rose." "Wynonna" means "first daughter" and "Rose" is my daughter's middle name.

Well, the "Wynonna Rose" and I didn't seem to get off to a good start. She did, however, teach me a lot about engines. Coming from a crab fisherman out in Maryland, what attracted me to this vessel was the open deck it had that would be ideal for pulling nets, and the space to install a hydraulic net lifter.

I knew from the start, getting the vessel from Maryland to Michigan was going to be a challenge, but I didn't let that stop me. The seller was willing to meet halfway in Ohio. After the exchange, it wasn't more than 10 miles on the interstate that I had a tire blowout. Okay, these things happen. Unfortunately for me, they happen all the time, especially on Sundays when no businesses are open. So, I took a rachet strap and secured the rim as close as I could to the frame of the trailer, and slowly continued to an off-ramp. I found an auto parts store that agreed to let me leave the boat in their secure parking lot for the night. The next morning when I went back, nothing was missing. The boat was still there. Once the boat was back in Michigan, it wasn't long before I had it in the water and the boys were back to pulling nets.

Not far into the season, I realized my plans for the summer of 2021 weren't going to work out as I hoped. I had the Wynonna Rose in the water, I had my boys pulling nets with me, and I was supplying the food trailer with fish. But my bad luck struck again when the engine problems started. The engine overheated and cracked a head. I'm no mechanic, nor do I have the space available to do work on such a  massive engine. I am, however, a problem solver. So, with a come-along, a sturdy tree branch, and an ambitious sidekick, I removed the engine from the Wynonna Rose.

After I replaced the head and put the engine back together, I discovered more water in my engine oil. Not sure if it was a mistake I had made while replacing the head, and not getting a good seal, or if the block was cracked, I ordered a new engine block with the heads already attached. I pulled parts of the old engine and put them on the new one. This of course wasn't until I made several attempts to correct the problem and put a lot of resources towards fixing it. I thought starting fresh  would solve the problem. But of course, after replacing the engine block and several parts, I discovered the problem originally was with the heat exchanger for the internal cooling system. This exchanger had a small hole that allowed radiator fluid to leak out and allow lake water to access the engine. So, when I put this old part on my new engine, it created the same overheating problems and contaminated my engine oil with water all over again.

This was so frustrating. I had to listen to criticism from friends and family about how my hopes and dreams of getting to the point of self-sufficient sustainability with my business wouldn't work. Eager to succeed, I turned to some of the other fishermen in the tribe.

 So, for the 2022 fishing season, I decided to lease out my fishing nets. The idea was to allow others to use my nets, in exchange for them providing me with 50 percent of their total catch. This was the quickest way I could think of to

get fish into my food trailer in order to make sales. Through the ups and downs of the 2022 fishing season, I would say this move saved my butt.

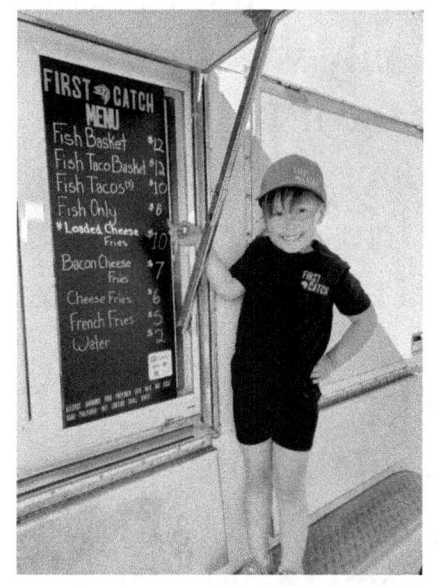

This temporary solution allowed me to focus on the food trailer and schedule events around the area. I was able to spend the intended time I wanted with my family. My younger children quickly became acclimated to food trailer life. My older boys had mixed feelings. They enjoyed the activities happening at the events rather than working in the trailer. However, when they needed or wanted money, they were quick to bargain for their "services rendered." This came in the form of babysitting their younger siblings or taking food orders at the service window. Regardless, the system wasn't perfect, but the time spent with the family was worth it for me.

I believe one of the unspoken heroes from my previous season is my nephew, Ethan. I would say Ethan committed himself more to the trailer than my two older children did, which seemed to work out for everyone. He has expressed interest in continuing to work for me next season and is eager to be part of the operation in any way that he can.

My daughter naturally became my quality control advisor. She made sure the fish was good enough for kids to eat. Not only was she focused on the fish, but she was also super excited about the cheese fries I served from the trailer. The story with the cheese fries: in an attempt to increase sales, it was my daughter's mother, my "insignificant other," Ali, who suggested adding cheese sauce to the menu to create a combination of cheese fries. This was a big hit. At certain events, they sold faster than the fish. At the powwow in Baraga, MI, my cousin told me he saw about 1 out of every 3 kids walking by his concession stand holding my cheese fries. Congratulations Ali, s-point for you.

As the family bounced from event to event for the summer of 2022, I still had concerns about the fishing. I knew I was being shorted my share of the catch. However, I did what I could to make it work.

With the current fish processing facility now in place, and the lack of access to the resource with the Wynonna Rose being sidelined by engine problems, I knew I needed to make another change. Some of my family strongly advised against it. Telling a Smith they can't do something is bound to end in them proving you wrong, so, I started researching how to expand First Catch.

New beginnings: I kept the idea of fishing and made cycling as many fish as possible through the food trailer my priority. However, I understood that time management between fishing and the food trailer was going to be a severe challenge. So, I decided I was going to focus most of my time on fishing for the upcoming season in 2023, and start looking for markets to buy at wholesale. The food trailer would be scaled back to be more of a hobby, as I still wanted to continue to see this succeed, and I have established a following over the last few years. I can't let down my fans! Katrina was no longer my partner in crime with the food trailer, but being that she was a Hospitality Management major in college, she taught me a lot. Thankfully, Ali has stepped up and was the major contributing factor to the overall success of this past season for the food trailer.

I knew if I was going to take another shot at making First Catch what it had the potential to be when I first started, I needed to talk to my brother, Joe. Just as before, it didn't take much convincing. Joe has spent the last 5-6 years working for a company, painting water towers. Joe told me he would rather be pulling gill nets than swinging 150-ft. off the ground, swiping paint on a tower as the wind blew him past it.

The search for a bigger vessel began. In the past, tribal fishermen would focus on either trap netting or gill netting to harvest fish. In the history of our tribal fishery, there has only been one operation that used trap nets for harvesting fish. My idea was to outfit a vessel that would be able to do both at the same time. Our tribal laws allow for fishermen to set 12,000ft (about 3.66 km) of gill net at one time, or 12 trap nets at one time. Historically, tribal fishermen would choose gill nets. I wanted to do both. Every time I go back to the "drawing board" to rethink my business strategy, I come up with something different.

This would include getting away from the cutthroat restaurant sales by implementing the food trailer, leasing fishing equipment to stay in the game when I had engine problems, and now, purchasing a vessel that can manage gill nets and trap nets on the same trip.

This time, I was fortunate enough to find a vessel closer to me than Maryland. For the upcoming season, I plan on using the fishing vessel "Norska" in Lake Superior. This boat was previously owned by the Bailey's Harbor Fish Company in Northern Wisconsin. The owners of Bailey's Harbor Fish Company have been very accommodating and very understanding throughout the sale of the vessel. They were even gracious enough to include the equipment I needed to start fishing at a larger scale than in previous seasons. I am very excited to see how the next season turns out.

In closing, I am reminded of those first words from Neil, "So, you wanna be a fisherman hey?" I often look back on all the struggles and challenges I have tackled so far. I took the initiative to create a fishing operation, to be the first in my generation to focus on breaking away from the normal aspects of working for the "man" or having a sense of job security. My focus, or what is important to me, is the quality of time I spend with my children. I also want to be the first to create a teaching platform to share with other potential fishermen in the tribal community, the first to educate others about our shared relation with fishing, our Native American culture, the first to create a fishing charter service concept that is specifically oriented towards commercial and subsistence fishing for the community, and the first to establish a "trade-school" concept for others to learn from. Hence the name of my fishing operation, "First Catch." So, to answer your question Neil…yes! Yes, I do wanna be a fisherman, my friend. Thank you.

CHRIS PETERSEN

I had several lengthy conversations with Chris Petersen while putting together his family's history in Great Lakes commercial fishing.

Chris Petersen, Picking Chubs

Ben Petersen slugging nets

Chris's great-grandfather, Ole Petersen, immigrated from Norway in 1866 and started farming in Fountain, Michigan.

Then in 1927, Chris's Grandfather, Ben, moved his family to Muskegon, where he started fishing. They first started fishing from rowboats, but they eventually bought a combination Gill-netter Trap-net boat, the 30-foot *"Seagull."*

Chris' grandfather, Ben Petersen was a very capable, practical man: An inventor and even a licensed steam engineer at the Muskegon Waterworks. This all worked in his favor when he was trying to start a new, commercial fishing business. Ben had five sons, and three of them fished with their father: Richie, Jim, and Chris's father, Ken (now 93 years old!). Chris's brother, Alan, is also involved in the family fishing business, and his older brother, Bill, is the Chairman of the Board.

Ken & Jim Petersen

Ken Petersen reeling nets

In the 1940s, they bought a used, 1909 Burger-built boat, the *"Three Brothers"*.

Then in 1955, they self-built their first steel-hulled boat, called *"Oral,"* named after Chris's grandmother.

In 1960, Grandfather Ben died. Then Chris's Uncle Ritchie went into the trucking business, hauling fish from Muskegon down to Indiana.

The family then bought the wooden boat, "*Peter A*" in 1963. Chris's dad was going to re-bottom the "*Peter A*" for $7000 but instead bought another steel boat for $8000. That was the "*Maggie Lynn*", another Burger-built boat.

The Oral was replaced by the 48-foot Burger-built boat, the "*Margaret Matthews*".

FISHING AS A 10-YEAR-OLD

As for Chris, he started fishing in 1972 with his Uncle Jim at age nine. Chris said they wanted a good deckhand, better known as a slave!

In 1974, Chris was 10 years old and Chris's dad sent him along with his Uncle Jim to help pull nets over at Sheboygan Reef. It was a beautiful day, a 4-hour run each way, and Chris enjoyed the day, except that he had to dress all the fish after they pulled the nets (the youngest crewman's job). On the way home, Chris was investigating the boat. The *"Margaret Matthews"* had a tall stack behind the pilothouse and there were two Kahlenberg air horns mounted on top of that stack.

After seeing the rest of the boat, Chris thought that sitting on top of those horns, well above the rest of the boat, was a good spot to sit and enjoy the view on such a nice day. After a while, the engines slowed and Chris heard his uncle yell, "Do you see him?" His Uncle Jim had come out of the wheelhouse and was looking aft with his binoculars.

Chris spoke, asking his uncle, "What are we looking for?" It scared Uncle Jim half to death. His uncle looked up and saw Chris sitting on the horns and said, "I was looking for an excuse to give your dad that I had lost you over the side. Next time you decide to sit up there, would you please tell somebody!" Chris thought he might get his butt beat, but his uncle was maybe too relieved to punish him.

FISHING FULL TIME

In 1977, Chris fished with Richard McNabb for chubs out of Muskegon. This was because the chub fishing licenses had been limited by the DNR, and the Petersens did not get one of the five licenses. During that period, in 1978, Chris's brothers fished in Lake Superior with the VanLandschoots

Chris & Alan Petersen, Lifting Trap Nets

out of Munising, and they decided to come back home to fish with a trap-net boat, which they had learned from fishing on Lake Superior.

Their Trap-Net boat, "Chet"

So, in 1990, the three brothers decided to build their own boat, a 52-foot steel boat called the "Petersen Bros." It launched in 1992, and they still own it. All three brothers were good welders, but they were also trying to fish at the same time. So, it took close to twenty months to build the boat.

Chris said there is a sense of elation when the keel is laid, which turns to depression while framing the boat. But when the hull is finished, another period of elation sets in, soon to head back to depression while installing the machinery and outfitting the boat.

ANOTHER BOAT NEEDED

Then came the "Buddy B," which they bought in 1998. The "Buddy B" was wrecked and on the beach. Looking back, Chris said it might have been cheaper to start from scratch. However, it turned out to be a good boat and they still fish with that boat today.

TEAMING UP WITH A FRIEND

Chris has been friends with Eric Anderson for most of their lives. In 2004, Chris had just strung a new set of 2-5/8" chub nets. He went out with Eric on the "Maggie Lynn" to pull eight boxes of nets. That pull ended up with 1000 pounds of fish, which wasn't too

bad. Eric asked Chris, "So, do you want to wet those new nets?" and Chris agreed.

They went north to set those nets and set six boxes of new nets, plus three boxes of the old nets, before hearing that the weather was turning bad. They returned the next day to pull those three boxes of new nets and three boxes of the old nets, which had only been in the water just overnight. To their surprise, they had another 1000-pound catch.

Chris and Eric Anderson

Then in 2011, Chris was having dinner in Coronado, California, when his friend Eric Anderson called again. Eric said he had found anti-freeze in his oil pan (cracked block), and he wasn't able to continue fishing. Chris came home and he bought the "Sheryl Dennis" out of Manistique, Chris strung some new nets, and he fished with Eric for whitefish out of Sand Bay. The two continued to team up the next year, fishing for whitefish out of Sand Bay, in Door County, Wisconsin. However, that venture wasn't profitable and they only fished for one season. Hoping to make their fortune in the lucrative fall fishing in Green Bay, that year was the worst on record and they only sold their 10-day catch for $638.

A man from Munising wanted to buy the "*Sheryl Dennis*" sight unseen, so Chris sold it. He bought another 40-foot, Burger-built boat, the "*Peggy S*", over the objections of his wife, and Chris returned to Door County in May 2012. The "*Peggy S*" was renamed the 'JR Petersen". They had minor success and decided to return to Bailey's Harbor in the fall to fish on the Lake side, leaving the "Peggy S" moored at the Hickey Bros.' dock.

When Chris returned after Thanksgiving to start fishing, he encountered one of the lowest water levels the Great Lakes had seen, and his boat was sitting on the bottom. Dennis Hickey asked Chris if he wanted to make some money in Door County, and Chris answered, "I would if my boat wasn't sitting on the bottom." Dennis said, "Why don't you just sell me your boat and go home." So, Chris ended up selling the boat to Dennis Hickey.

I asked Chris to share some of his memories of unusual occurrences from his family's years of fishing:

LEG CRUSHED

One was from his pre-fishing days when he was about 4 or 5 years old. His father, Ken, saw their Uncle Jim flagging them down while out fishing in December. Jim's Kahlenberg engine was having problems, and he asked Ken to bring him some parts for repairs. The two boats came next to each other, and Chris's father got his leg crushed between the two boats.

He was helped to get home. At first, he said he'd be okay, but Chris remembered his dad sitting on his toy box, trying to recover. Finally, his dad decided he'd better go to the hospital. The leg was not broken, but had major muscle and tissue damage, resulting in a blood clot that went to Ken's lung.

Chris remembered that this bad event did result in the best Christmas he'd ever had, because many neighbors, even people they hardly knew, dropped off Christmas gifts for the kids, knowing that the accident would affect the family's finances over the Holidays.

SUNKEN SKIFF

In 2012, Chris was fishing with his brother and nephew, pulling trap nets late in the season. The lake was very calm when they left that morning, and they pulled their nets without any problem. They were resetting their nets when the weather turned bad and started to blow 50 knots.

As they started to head in, a wall of water hit the pilothouse and went over the top of them, filling their skiff, which they were towing behind the tug. They pulled the skiff up close to the stern, but when shortened up, the line snapped, and the skiff sank. They figured it was lost and they went home.

A week later, they had a diver along and he found the skiff. The diver hooked a line to the skiff and the tug was able to pull the skiff up to the surface. Chris said it looked like a submarine bow breaking the surface. As they towed it toward home, it self-bailed.

GREATEST CHUB LIFT EVER

In 2003, chub fishing was fantastic, but in fast decline. Chris's dad had predicted, "That is going to be the end of it," when they started seeing the quagga mussels covering the food beds where the chubs would eat.

Chris had nets set just six miles offshore of Muskegon, and he and his two brothers were pulling the nets, with a very meager catch. His youngest brother said they should just reset the nets at the same place because it was close to home. Chris had heard from an old-timer about a good place offshore of Grand Haven, and he wanted to set the nets there. His older brother told him to do what he wanted, so Chris headed south to Grand Haven.

They set eight boxes of nets at the site where Chris had been told to set them. That was on Thursday, and on Sunday, their catch was 3000 pounds of chubs. They continued to have great success in that location for the rest of that season, so they returned the following year. They caught almost nothing that next season! The chubs were gone!

PERCH FISHING

In November 1983, Chris was contacted by his old friend, Gary Diepenhorst, who was from Saugatuck, Michigan. Gary wanted someone to fish with him for perch in Indiana waters.

On November 10th, Chris and Gary were on the 45-foot gill-netter, the "*Shirly B*" out of Indiana Harbor, next to Chicago. They had set 13 boxes when another boat told them that it was about to blow, but Gary ignored the warning. When they finally decided to head in, they were caught in 15-20 foot seas, the worst Chris said he has ever experienced. At one point, Gary told Chris, "We're so high up, I can see a lady in the Sears Tower sharpening her pencil." The winds were coming from due north, and Gary told Chris that those waves were coming from the Mackinac Bridge. In fact, Chris said they were still encountering 6-foot waves inside the Calumet Harbor breakwater. They were forced into the Calumet River because of a bridge closure in Indiana Harbor. They returned later to pull their nets and had not lost any during the storm.

KNOW WHEN TO SAY NO

In 1985, Chris received a call to fish with the crew of the tug "*Searcher*" out of Chicago. He had heard things about that boat that made him uncomfortable, so he turned down the offer.

In December of that year, the vessel sank, and three of the six crewmen were lost.

The picture shows the "Searcher" under its previous name. "L.P. Hill".

SUMMARY

Chris continues to fish with his nephews. They jokingly call themselves Larry, Moe (that's Chris!) & Curly. They like fishing together and they have fun, but they work safely and efficiently. When not fishing, Chris continues to string and repair nets for other fishermen. Chris sells all of his catch to other processors, so he doesn't have the stress of preparing the fish and making retail sales, which most fishermen will say that they hate.

Chris said that one time he was out fishing with his two nephews and brother Bill, and Chris took a tumble, falling on the deck. One nephew started laughing and the other one asked what was so funny. When they told him that Chris had taken an awkward fall, the nephew that missed it said, "Hey, do it again. I missed it." Chris answered, "Hey, we have an adult along," referring to his 72-year-old brother, Alan.

Chris credits his grandfather for the family's success. Grandpa Ben was not extravagant and refused to get a loan to buy a good boat, the "*Mallard*" for $4500. Instead, he built the "*Oral*" himself. He said he didn't want his friends and neighbors to see him in the bank, because they might think poorly of him. Ben said, "I'll save the stocks for my grandsons," and Chris said his grandpa would roll over in his grave over the money he spent to build his home, knowing what the old family homestead was like.

Left to right standing, Joel (Alan's son), Eric (Bill's son), & Bill. Seated, Alan and Chris

Chris says he has no regrets for just doing what he loves for a living, and I'm sure he will continue to fish for many years to come. They are now fishing with the "Peterson Bros." and the "Buddy B". In the off-season, Chris repairs nets for other fishermen, and he and his nephews string new nets as well.

TWO RIVERS, WISCONSIN FISHING MUSEUM

The Rogers Street Fishing Village & Museum in Two Rivers has a wonderful collection of fishing memorabilia, boats, Kahlenberg Diesel engines, as well as other maritime-related collections. The museum staff graciously

permitted their photos to be used in this book, such as the old "*Susie-Q*" originally owned by their neighbor, Susie-Q Fisheries, where I have bought fish for over 35 years.

This replica of an old Mackinaw fishing boat is located at the Two Rivers Museum.

The museum has a large collection of Kahlenberg diesel engines, some still runnable.

The Kahlenberg Company is located in Two Rivers and is not only known for its diesel engines, which needed to have the cylinder heads heated with small blow torches in order to get them started in cold weather. Kahlenberg's reputation is worldwide because of their famous, Kahlenberg air horns, which have a distinctive, low bellowing noise on the large ship models, known by Great Lakes boat watchers when they hear the Captain's salutes

at locations like the Soo Locks and Duluth Harbor. Propellers, propeller shafts, and other maritime products are also made to high, Kahlenberg standards. If you are a Hockey fan and attend games at large, NHL arenas, you may also like to know that many of those loud horns you hear at those games in some arenas are also produced by Kahlenberg air horns.

The Buddy-O was built as a gill-netter in 1936 and fished until it sank in 1976. It was raised and is now listed in the National Maritime Initiative's Register of Preserved Historic Vessels.

The following photo is from the Jim Legault collection:

JIM LEGAULT PHOTOGRAPHY

Jamie LeClair put me in contact with Jim Legault, who is well-known in Commercial Fishing circles for his great action shots of the boats, the men, and real-life fishing photos. I recognized the Legault name and found out that Jim was the grandson of my neighbor, when I was growing up over in Marinette, Wisconsin. Jim has graciously permitted me to use the following photographs from his collection.

HENRICKSEN FISHING, SISTER BAY, WI

Trap Net boat, with open deck. The design is to allow the Trap Net to be pulled over the side until the Pot is alongside, and then the fish are dipped from the pot and into the boat.

Charlie & Will Hendricksen and crew

Dipping the catch out of the Trap net

Hickey Bros., Bailey's Harbor Fish Company

I'm using Jim Legault's pictures, which he took at Hickey Brothers. However, I was asked to survey one of their older fish tugs recently, during the writing of this book. You will see that tug in the **"First Catch"** section, with Paul Smith's story.

Todd Stuth allowed me to use the following history from their web page:

The Hickey Family began fishing in Baileys Harbor in the mid-1800s. Martin Hickey Sr. began fishing hooks for Lake Trout using a wooden 20' flat bottom boat. He purchased his first boat in the Late 1800s (Burger boat 19) and named it the Pathfinder. Martin was also a partner with the Brann Bros. (owned the local general store in Baileys Harbor) and was also a partner in a sailing schooner. The schooner would haul Martin's fish, cordwood, and telegraph poles from North Bay to Milwaukee. The return trip brought Brann's general store merchandise.

William and Martin Hickey Jr. (sons of Martin Sr.) were the next generation of fishermen in Baileys Harbor. They began fishing gill nets and pond nets in the early 1900s. The Hickey's dock existed where the current Baileys Harbor Town Marina is today.

Dennis and Jeffrey Hickey (sons of William) are the 3rd-generation of fishermen in Baileys Harbor. They began working with CJ Winegar fishing alewives in the 1960s after duty in the US Navy. After two years of working for Winegar, he was ready to retire, so they purchased his fishing rig and quota. They moved their operations to the other side of the harbor where the Baileys Harbor Yacht Club Condos are located today. In the 1970s, they purchased a gill net boat and named it the Pathfinder in honor of their grandfather and father. The pond net boat the Leif was their next boat. Fishing operations grew steadily into the 1980s.

In 1985, Dennis and Jeff moved a small garage onto their property. This became their first fish processing plant. They moved the original retail store from Jeff's garage on Hwy 57 (run by Jeff's wife Patricia) to this building as well. The brothers worked to grow the wholesale of fish to Chicago & New York and then began exporting fish and caviar to the Scandinavian countries in the 1990s. At this time they purchased the Anclam Rd property and constructed a dock-the current home port for all of Hickey Bros Research/Baileys Harbor Fish Company vessels.

Over the years, Hickey Bros has worked with the Wisconsin DNR, Sea Grant, Fisheries Coop at UW-Stevens Point, and US Fish & Wildlife to complete numerous assessments, tagging, and research projects. This resulted in Dennis Hickey's appointment by Governor Tony Earl to the Great Lakes Fish Commission-Lake Michigan Commercial Fisheries Advisor, a position that he still holds today.

In 2000, Dennis Hickey's daughter Carin (Hickey) Stuth and son-in-law Todd Stuth became actively involved in the fishery after finishing college degrees. Carin and Todd have grown the brand to include Baileys Harbor Fish Company and remodeled the processing plant to have the retail fish shop facing the road. The fleet of boats has grown to accommodate the fishing in both the Bay of Green Bay and Lake Michigan. We have expanded the research projects that Hickey Bros. Research LLC completed beyond Wisconsin and into the inland Northwest US. We are proud to continue the commercial fishing tradition in Door County and the Wisconsin waters of Lake Michigan and the bay of Green Bay.

The older model

vs. The Modern fish tugs

Much of the Hickey Bros. fishing is done off the Great Lakes, but they are also fishing invasive species in the lakes within the National Parks, such as Yellowstone.

Massey Fish Co., St. Ignace, Michigan

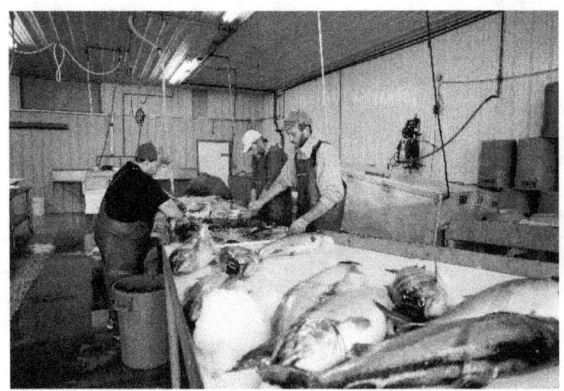

Peterson, Fairport Fisheries, Fairport, Michigan

VanLandschoot & Sons, Munising, Michigan

Weborg Fisheries, Gills Rock, Wisconsin

STORMS, WRECKS, AND DANGERS

Pat Kinney, who fishes on eastern Lake Superior, tells the story about spending the night on a small island in Whitefish Bay, Lake Superior on the night that the Edmund Fitzgerald went down. He was eighteen at the time and is still fishing. Four other fishermen sank their boats, it was a "bad wind," Pat said.

Drew Purvis (see the following, Purvis Fisheries History) also tells the story about the night when the Fitzgerald sank. They had 1-inch cables tied from the boats to trees up on the hill with complete engine blocks on the cables to try and take the surge. When the cables came tight, the engine blocks would just spin on the cables. He said it was wild to watch, and he hasn't seen wind at their dock like that since that time, and they hope they never see it again.

Clancy Fuller related a story about his grandfather, Fred Fuller, and his dad, Everett (Sonny) Fuller, and Johnny Schiller, who were caught in a storm on 21 March 1955. Their fish tug sank on Old Hen Island, and they stayed in a cabin overnight until a search plane found them the next morning. They were then taken off the island by another fish tug. (See the pictures which follow).

Clancy's story was told as follows:

"Skipper Fred Fuller and his deck hands, Everett 'Sonny' Fuller, his son, and Johnny Schiller left Kingsville Harbour before daylight, like any normal day of fishing on the 28-foot Beachcomber. The winds and seas began to pick up as they reached their nets, and they began to pull their nets. The radio began to crackle with the news that other boats were cutting and running back to the harbour. The gale winds began to pick up, with waves averaging 30 to 40 feet.

The crew headed back to the harbour, which was about an hour's run. About 15 minutes from the safe haven of home, a comber hit the Beachcomber, crashing into a gangway and ripping the stove off the wall, knocking Sonny out for a few minutes. The skipper turned the Beachcomber's head into the waves to help upright the vessel, and he decided to head for Pelee Island until the winds died down. With the waves crashing against the tug, and with blinding snow, the vessel was blown off course.

When Old Hen Island appeared, the captain was able to sail the Beachcomber into the small harbour, although the opening was only a couple feet wider than his boat. As soon as they hit the beach, the Beachcomber sank, and the crew broke the ice off the skipper's hands, which were still on the ship's wheel. They climbed through the front window of the tug and broke into a small hunting cabin on the island for shelter.

The townspeople sat at the end of the dock in Kingsville with their headlights on, just in case the small vessel made it back that night. The next morning, the Windsor Star Newspaper rented a search plane and found the crew on the island. A fish tug named the RAYMARBEV went the same day and rescued the crew to be united with their families. Here are a few pictures of the Beachcomber and crew."

Families waiting for the rescued fishermen.

Damage to Kingsville Harbor from the storm.

Gail Cromwell Noyes told me about her father, Lionel Taylor Cromwell, and a young relative of theirs on his tug. His tug boat was in Port Stanley, Ontario. She recalls her father telling her stories about when he had gone on a few search and rescue trips on Lake Erie due to bad weather. Because the fishermen were scattered over Lake Erie most days of the week, they were better positioned for a quick response, search, and rescue, than the Coast Guard was in many instances. Gail gave me copies of two letters sent to her father, thanking him for his efforts to locate their relatives. He operated that tug until 1951 when we moved to East Alton, Illinois, to work on the Mississippi Barge Lines out of St. Louis. "I think the move was encouraged by my Uncle Clarence G. Cromwell, who had moved there first. Life was a bit easier than the storms of Lake Erie," Gail said.

Gail also said, "I loved to go to the shanty and watch the fishermen mend nets or what other chores they had to do there, but my mom never wanted me there due to the language of the seamen. One thing that sticks in my mind, is my dad telling me what a rough sea it could be out on the Lake, and eating cold beans out of a can for their meal. He said he had fallen overboard once and never even knew how to swim, but all was well, and he was rescued quickly. My brother Clarence Ashley Cromwell also worked on the water for a while when he was younger." Gail sent the pictures and clippings in this story.

Gail also told me about a fellow named Shaun Vary, who came from a fishing family, but he now sails Great Lakes cargo ships. Shaun contacted me and sent stories and pictures.

LEGISLATION PROBLEMS

In Wisconsin, legislation started to affect commercial fishing as early as 1885. Even the Wisconsin fishery in Lake Superior has different regulations. There is a quota system for fishing Cisco, but whitefish is regulated by restrictions on the gear used to fish for them. There are eleven state licenses, plus Tribal Fishery, with a set number of trap nets that can be set per license. There is also a limit to the number of feet of gill net that can be set, and only a certain number of Lake Trout can be harvested as a bycatch in whitefish gill nets. And maybe even fear

In the 1980s, the number of new licenses was limited to discourage part-time fishermen, hoping that the full-time fishermen would be better invested and be more successful.

Lake Michigan and Green Bay have different regulations in Wisconsin waters, limiting the number of perch and whitefish that can be caught. and each State and Province surrounding the Great Lakes also sets their own regulations. In 1996, perch fishing was closed on Lake Michigan because populations had declined drastically.

Is there any wonder that Commercial Fishermen are frustrated and maybe even fear their State DNR?

ENVIRONMENTAL PROBLEMS

Pollution has been a problem for commercial fishing for many years. Then came the invasive species: lamprey eels, alewives, zebra mussels, and now the quagga mussels.

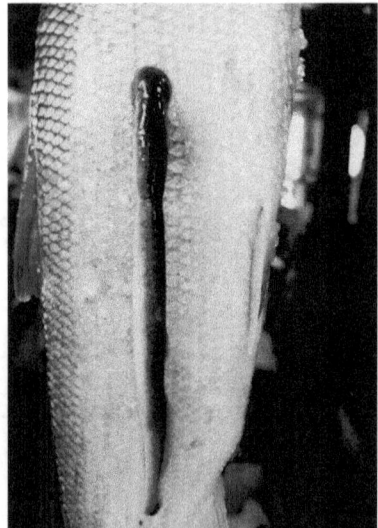

Jim Legault photos

Surprisingly, one fish that has dealt well with the quagga mussel is the Lake Michigan whitefish. The whitefish actually eat the quagga, as well as midge larva, and even Round Goby. These foods may not be as nutritious as their preferred diet of Diporeia (an invertebrate) but at least the whitefish is surviving.

Sea Grant Photo

PURVIS FISHERIES

Purvis Fisheries was established in 1882 on Manitoulin Island, on the Canadian side of Lake Huron, George Purvis is the 4th-generation of the family, and his son, Drew Purvis is the 5th generation. There is a young, 6th generation coming along.

Purvis has a dock-side plant that houses several modern processing machines, allowing them to maximize quality and minimize waste. The dock-side location provides them the ability to process their catches immediately after the boats unload their catch; retaining as much freshness as possible.

Purvis uses both gill and trap nets. They sail two full-time 75-foot, 4-man crew gill net tugs, six days a week, March through January, and two 45-foot trap net boats, gathering their catch twice weekly. They also have two full-time employees who mend nets daily.

GILL NETTING

Gill netting is a selective means of catching fish you want to market. The size of the mesh, web strength, and net length and depth, regulate the size of the captured fish, so there is an extremely low incidence of bycatch, or non-target species (fish not intended for sale). Nets are made of monofilament web, which Purvis imports from Japan and China. The name 'gill' net refers to the means of capture - the fish are unable to squeeze their bodies through the mesh openings, and so are captured in this position because their gills prevent them from backing out of the netting. This effectively traps them. Fish smaller than the target fish simply swim through the net, and the larger ones effectively 'bang into' the net and change direction, avoiding capture.

The "Purvis" (gill net boat, Burnt Island Docks, 2009)

TRAP NETTING

Trap netting is much like you would guess, with one important distinction, it's a live trap; the fish are enclosed in an open volume of netting called a 'pot' and remain alive and able to swim and feed till the trap is raised to the surface. Unlike other animal traps, these nets are not baited; their success depends on the fish swimming into the trap and not being able to find their way out. During harvest, the fish are sorted and those which are not wanted, because of either their size or species, are returned to the water alive. This form of fishing requires patience and great knowledge of local waters while placing nets. The trap-net enclosure, fundamental to this form of harvest, allows for a catch of unmatched freshness.

Trap Net Boat (Burnt Island Docks, 2009)

A STORIED HISTORY

The Purvis Fisheries story begins in 1851 when William Purvis and his two brothers ventured from Arbroath Scotland, a fishing port still known as the home of the famous Arbroath Smokies (smoked fish). The three sailed to Canada, landing in the province of Quebec, and made their way to Hamilton, Ontario. They then started northwest through Guelph, west to Goderich, eventually reaching Kincardine, a port town on Lake Huron - this last stretch of their voyage was made on foot through the almost 50 km of undeveloped woodland.

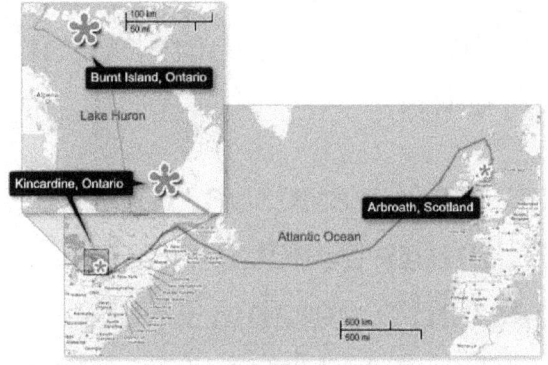

The journey from Arbroath, Scotland to Kincardine, Ontario, Canada.

William Purvis worked in Kincardine both as police chief and for a political party, and in 1872 was appointed the first lighthouse keeper at Great Duck Island - only 13 miles from the present Purvis Fisheries location. The records show that by 1882, William had started to fish commercially using a Mackinaw sailboat. He built his first steam tug in 1887 and his five sons were soon helping him fish the waters around Great Duck Island. The fish were packed in ice and salt and shipped by boat to Detroit for sale.

Purvis Brothers partnership, circa 1930
From left to right... William, John (Jack), James, Alexander, and Edward.

The present Purvis operation at Burnt Island was established in 1920 when Alexander, along with his three sons, moved their operations from Great Duck Island. Alexander and his sons George and Leonard fished from Burnt Island, and the third son Harold fished from Meldrum Bay. The fish were still shipped by boat, but to Cheboygan, Michigan rather than Detroit, and then by rail to Chicago, Illinois, beginning in 1946.

In 1962, George Purvis Jr., Alexander's grandson, took over Purvis Brothers. Ltd. Like all multi-generational businesses, the fishery has experienced a notable evolution over the years; from shipping products by water and rail in ice harvested from Lake Huron, to shipping the fish packed in man-made ice on refrigerated trucks; from fishing in a Mackinaw sailboat to steam tugs to fishing with diesel tugs; from operating free of electricity and modern roadways to functioning with modern equipped facilities. One constant over the last 80 years can be seen in the Purvis' company logo, the Blue Fin.

Designed and built by Alexander Purvis, the tug "Purvis" is still hard at work fishing six days a week. Purvis also proudly emulates the Arbroath Smokies of the 1850s in their own smoked fish products.

George Purvis Jr.'s two children, Drew and Denise, have recently taken over the family business - now in its fifth generation - and have created a sales division called Purvis Fisheries Inc.

The launch of "The Purvis", circa 2004
From left to right... Drew (with Denise's two children), Denise, and George.

SHAUN VARY

I met Shaun through the Internet during my search for Great Lakes Commercial Fishermen, while doing research for this book. Although Shaun is not a fisherman himself, he comes from 7-generations of Canadian commercial fishermen on Lakes Huron and Erie. He is a Great Lakes sailor, but Shaun does his best to keep the history of all the Canadian Lake Erie-style fish tugs alive, and he has self-published a couple of books on fish tugs (Google "Shaun Vary Collection" to see his photos). Shaun has a lot of friends who are fishermen, whom he put me in touch with. In fact, Shaun has a retired fishing tug (pictured below) that he is rebuilding in his spare time. She's a real beauty, and very representative of the older, Great Lakes fish tug style.

Shaun's sailing career started in 1987 when he attended Georgian College in Owen Sound, Ontario. After graduating, he took a shore job with Ontario Hydro, as it was near impossible to get a job aboard ship at the time, Shaun said. He worked ashore for about 9 years before going back to sailing, where he has worked for Algoma, Canada Steamship Lines, Lower

Lakes Towing (twice), and McKeil Marine (twice). He is now starting his 15th season as Chief Engineer in the 2022 season.

Shaun may not be an active Commercial Fisherman, but he deserves mention for his involvement in the industry.

Shaun Vary published a great story in the Port Dover, Ontario, Harbour Museum newsletter about the fishing tugboat named the **Aletha B.**, originally built in 1945.

Sunday, March 24, 1974, was to be a most tragic day for the familiar little fish tug. Dale Perry age 29, along with his brother Wayne age 20, were trawling for smelt approximately 16 kilometers southeast of Port Dover. A forty-knot wind was blowing, accompanied by building waves and snow squalls. The Perry brothers reported via VHF radio that they were done trawling for the day and heading home. **Aletha B.** suddenly capsized and soon afterward sank. Other tugs were in the area, including the **M & K**, captained by Alvin "Vinnie" Scott, and the **Trimac II** with Captain Terry Hagan in command. **Trimac II** responded, arriving in time only to see the overturned hull disappear beneath the waves. The tugs frantically searched for any signs of the Perry brothers, but they were not to be found. The two men were lost when the **Aletha B.** sank in approximately ninety feet of water. The fishing community along the north shore of Lake Erie mourned the loss caused by this tragedy.

Harry Gamble soon dispatched equipment to raise the sunken trawler, and she was hoisted to the surface of Lake Erie on April 25, 1974. **Aletha B.** was placed on a barge but ended up again in a sunken condition when the crane equipment failed. **Aletha B.** was being lifted from the barge, back into the water when this occurred. The Perry brothers were not located on board the tug as had been hoped, but their remains were recovered from the lake approximately a year later by two other Port Dover tugs. In a strange twist of fate, two brothers were to recover the Perry brothers. Captain Chuck Scott of the **Dover Rose** recovered Dale Perry in June of 1975, and Captain Vinnie Scott of the **M & K** recovered Wayne Perry in July of 1975.

Aletha B.'s sinking was determined to be the result of instability caused by overloading, or possibly ice build-up. She was tendered for sale in April of 1974 by the estate of Allen Dale Perry. After purchase and repair, **Aletha B.** went back to work in 1975 for George Gibbons. She continued the mundane yet honest trade of being a fish tug and was later purchased by Dave Ryerse. John Misner owned the vessel by 1980, and her days as a fish tug were soon over. The still useful hull was to become a workboat.

She now had the appearance of a small tugboat. She was a noted participant at 'Tugfest' in Penetanguishene Ontario, in the summer of 1990. At some point, the tug's name was changed to **Glen L.** and her commercial status was changed to that of a pleasure craft. The name change does not appear to be official, as the vessel remained listed as '**Aletha B.**' in the Transport Canada vessel registry. By 2000, **Glen L.**'s wheelhouse was raised one deck, giving a somewhat awkward and top-heavy appearance.

On Sunday, October 27, 2007, the **Glen L.** was transiting Georgian Bay with a destination of Midland, Ontario. On board was a crew of four, including Bryan Hogg, Donald Orange, Ronald Orange, and Shawn Orange. The tug began taking on water and capsized at a location given as 'four miles' from Byng Inlet, ON. The crew escaped to the water and made their way to an aluminium boat they had been towing. Sadly, one of the men, Donald Orange (age 65) of Port Hope Ontario, succumbed to the cold water and was lost. The **Glen L.** was not recovered and to this day, remains at the bottom of Georgian Bay.

Fishermen are noted to have superstitions regarding the boats that earn them a living on dangerous waters. It was seen to be a bad omen around the Port Dover waterfront when the **Aletha B.** fell off of her recovery barge and sank again. It may have been thirty-three years later and on a different body of water, but tragedy did revisit this former Lake Erie fish tug. It truly was bad luck for the **Glen L.**

OCONTO, WISCONSIN

One beautiful July day, I had the opportunity to meet with two of my West Shore of Green Bay fishermen/women, Nancy Swaer and Al Stranz. We first met for lunch at the Dockside Restaurant in Oconto, which is at the mouth of the Oconto River, where the fishing fleet had gathered back in the busy days. Bing Moes told Al Stranz that the herring fishery boomed in the late 1940s to mid-1950s when there were 50-60 tugs in Oconto in the fall. Al Stranz, who had fished with Bernard (Bing) Moes and Bing's son, Dave, from 1975-78 while going to college, was one of the ex-fishermen I met on this trip. More on Al's history and stories later in this chapter. Al pointed out the area across the street from the restaurant, where the Moes family fishery buildings had been located. That area is now parking for cars and boat trailers at the local marina.

One of our stops was at the Oconto County Court House to look at the High Relief sculpture design at the top of the building. The reason this was an important stop for this trip was to show how important two industries were to Oconto County, namely **FISHING** and **LOGGING**. Shipping was also a major industry in Oconto, but it was due to the other two industries. Note the relief showing the Great lakes Whitefish above the log in the following photos. It was meant to be much more than just a decoration on that building. Fishing was one of the major industries in this County.

Our next stop in Oconto was at the **Beyer Home & Carriage Museum**, where Al Stranz is on the Board of Directors for the Oconto County Historical Society. Al arranged for another Board member, Peter Stark, to meet us at the museum. Pete showed us the various displays in the museum, including many unusual fishing-related exhibits.

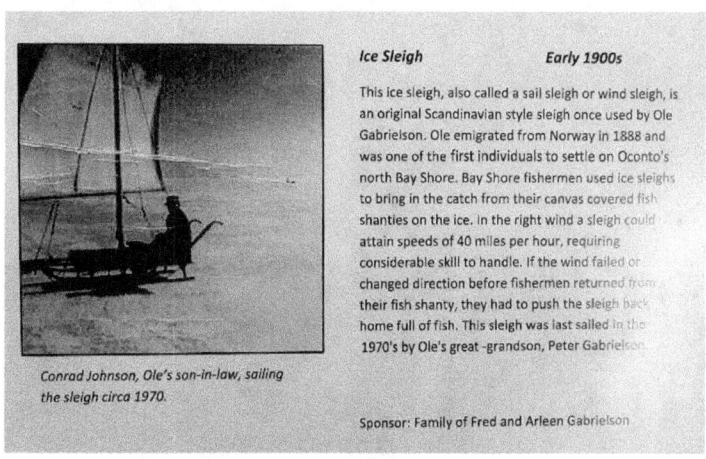

The following picture was taken in the museum, next to a '*sail sleigh' which was* used by the Gabrielson family for their ice fishing operation in the late 1800s. (Note the Bond Pickle Company sign in the background, which was another big Oconto Company). Nancy Swaer told me that she had worked at Bond Pickle in the summers of 1969-70, as well as a local shoe factory, before going to work with her dad, fishing in Green Bay. She said she was glad to get off the assembly lines and out on the water. Nancy added, that everybody in Oconto worked at Bond's at some point.

Commercial Fishermen - Great Lakes Style

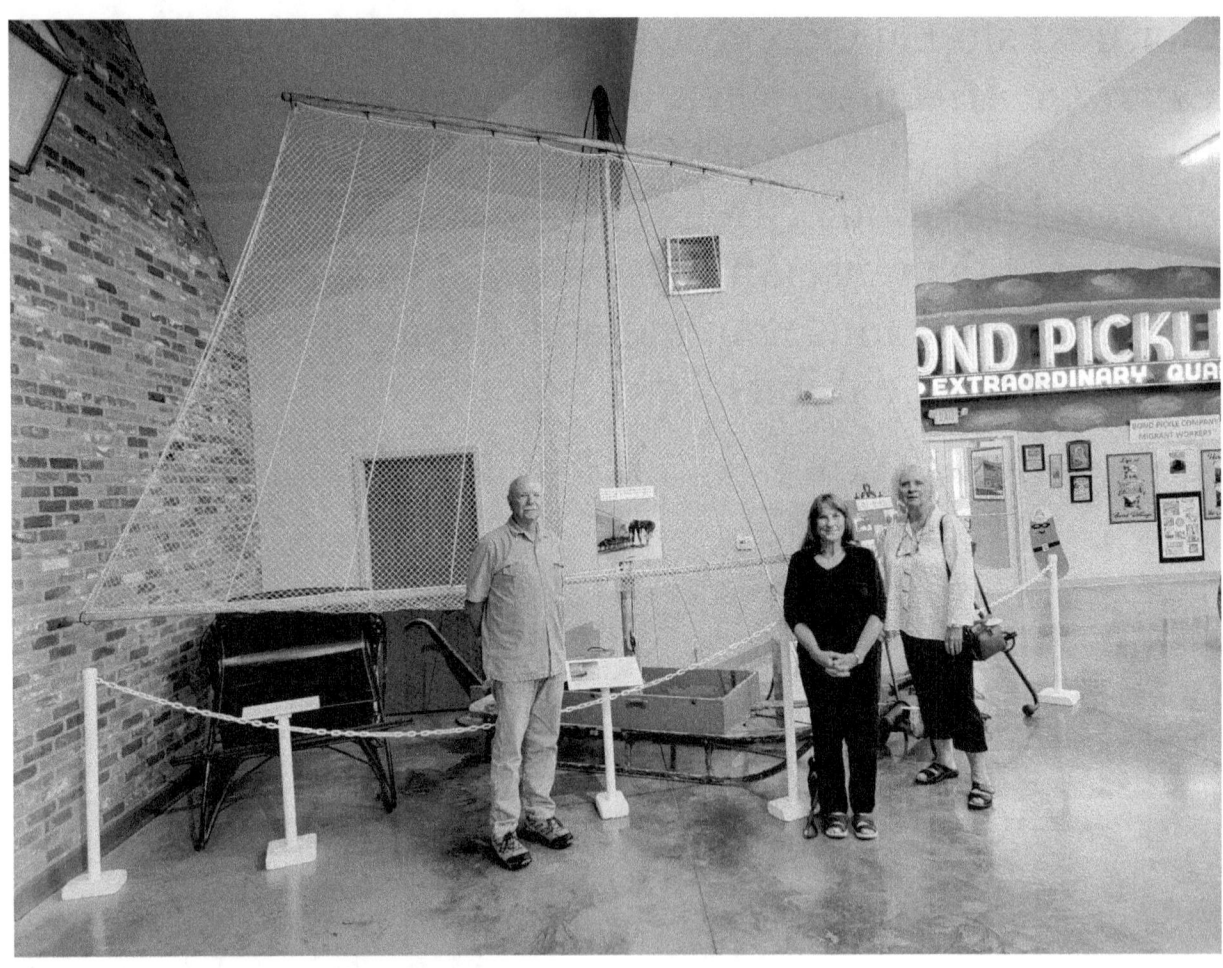

AL STRANZ

A little of my background: I worked for Bernard (Bing) Moes and his son Dave during my college years at UW-GB, 1975-78. I had known Bing and Dave for years (Dave and his wife were 2-3 years older than me) and I had stopped in their retail store numerous times for smoked fish.

I was a biology/environmental science major and thought that commercial fishing would be great experience. I even got some independent credits for a large fish collection I made one summer. That collection could still be in the UW-Green Bay lab. The majority of the fishing I did was on pound nets for alewife and smelt, but we also had fyke nets out for perch, and gill nets in the winter for whitefish and northern pike. Perch, smelt, whitefish, lawyer, and northern pike were sold through the fish house. Alewife all went to Art Swaer, either at the freezer plant on Frog Pond Road, south of Oconto or to Art's meal plant in Pensaukee.

Bing also smoked and sold a lot of fish. When I was there, he smoked 800-1000# of chubs every week or so, boxed them up in 2-½ pound boxes, and "fish peddlers" (a classic Oconto occupation) sold them all over the Midwest. The chubs came from fishermen out of Milwaukee. He used hard maple scraps from a bowling pin factory in Suamico to smoke them.

Some trivia: We hauled all the alewife in a 1958-9 tandem axel Ford dump truck with an early vintage automatic transmission. It would hold 22-23,000# of fish. When hauling to Pensaukee, once I turned south off Main St. in Oconto onto CTH-S I would put the gas pedal to the floor and hold it there to Pensaukee, reaching a top speed of somewhat less than 40 MPH.

Once reaching Pensaukee, we just dumped the fish on a concrete slab adjacent to the plant and the employees pushed them into an auger that ran into the cooker. One time, the cable that controlled the power take-off for the lift broke, and I had to shovel most of the 20,000# of alewife out of the box (the same ones we had just shoveled in). When I got back to the fish house in Oconto and explained the delay, Bing asked me if I knew every fish by name.

Bing had an old Lake Superior trap net boat for alewife. The last time I was in Pensaukee, the Della was onshore near the old meal plant. It was powered by an old Gray Marine flathead gas engine. They also had two open, approx. 25' v-hull steel boats, with 100-120HP outboards used for pulling fyke nets and carrying extra alewife. I almost sunk one of them coming in overloaded one morning when the bow wake from a large pleasure boat broke over the bow of my boat. I bailed water and fish until I reached the dock.

There was also a 16-17' steel flat-bottomed boat with a 33-HP Evinrude for going inside the pond nets when lifting. In the above picture of the Della, there is a long plank and crossways in the boat in the background. This plank was placed between the Della and the smaller boat that was inside the pond net. You crawled across the plank to get to the small boat to help "bag the net".

Gill netting in winter was done by snowmobile on early ice, or using a 1967 Ford, ¾-ton, 2 Wheel Drive.

The worst part of the job, in my opinion, was tarring the nets in the spring. We would string them all out in the field across the road from the fish house (where the parking lot is now), sew up any holes, and add floats or leads as needed. We would then stack them on a frame and, using a couple of old power poles and a winch, we dipped them in a large tank of hot net tar. Then we spread them all out again in the field. The worst thing that could happen would be if a rabbit or muskrat wandered into the field of nets and chewed more holes in them.

One time, Dave and I were lifting perch nets with one of the open boats off the County Park north of Oconto. When resetting the net, Dave backed up the boat under power while I held onto the net's anchor line until everything was tight. While backing up, under almost full power, the motor suddenly revved up. We looked back to see the propeller skipping across the water. Luckily, we had an extra prop in the boat, but no nut for the shaft. Using a hose clamp from the bilge pump and a cotter pin, we rigged it up well enough to limp the five-or-so miles back to the dock.

I worked for Bing and Dave until the fall of 1978. Bing died unexpectedly in early October and I helped Dave finish up the fall work. Soon after, Dave sold the business and licenses to Art and Dean Swaer

Al sent the following photos of a great old fish tug, the Maggie Jane, still fishing out of Oconto.

Jason Frazier lives in the Upper Peninsula of Michigan, and he told me, "I am a 5th generation fisherman on the Northern Great Lakes. I spent 31 years on the lakes. My family fished under State licenses until 1978 when we achieved our Native status. Jason has been writing memoirs, hoping to find someone to help put a book together about his family history. Jason's great-grandmother was born on High Island in 1871 and moved to St. James on Beaver Island in 1890 with her parents.

Her dad was a fisherman. Jason's family came up through Manitoulan Bay to St. Joseph Island, then to Hessel, MI, then to the Islands, and Seoul Chiox Point. Eventually, a lot of his family ended up at the Top of the Lake, where he now lives. Jason has been fishing around the Islands since 1980 but has been back working on Beaver Island for the last three and a half years doing concrete work.

ABOUT THE AUTHOR

Bob Ojala is an author, writing both non-fiction and fiction books, generally dealing with life in the maritime industry. His novels center around real-life events where possible, changing names and locations to protect privacy.

Bob Ojala has a BSE in Naval Architecture & Marine Engineering from the University of Michigan. Bob spent four years in the U.S. Coast Guard, 17 years with the American Bureau of Shipping, and 8-1/2 years with the U.S. Army Corps of Engineers, in addition to 30 years in his own business (including the time while with the USACE). Bob is still active in marine surveying.

Bob is a Wisconsin native with Finnish roots. His father was a Merchant Mariner for 32 years, giving Bob the interest in the Maritime Industry, but not the desire to be a sailor.

Bob worked as a Naval Architect, designing small passenger vessels, tugs, and barges after graduation. However, Bob found he enjoyed working in the shipyard, with the workers, more than sitting in the design office.

When the opportunity came to join the American Bureau of Shipping, working as a Field Surveyor, inspecting ships, and equipment going into shipbuilding, Bob thought this was what he was looking for.

Eventually, Bob started his own Marine Surveying & Consulting business. Because Great Lakes clients were slow in changing loyalties, Bob began traveling the world, surveying (inspecting) cruise ships, tankers, drydocks, historic vessels, and even some warships. Bob also performed investigations of accidents, pollution incidents, and several accidental deaths.

Bob always wanted to document the lives of commercial fishermen on the Great Lakes because he had lived on the shores of Green Bay while growing up, which had many commercial fishermen in the Menekaunee (Marinette) and Peshtigo, Wisconsin, harbors. Some of Bob's childhood friends came from fishing families, and Bob watched the fishermen set nets trough the ice during the winter. Bob even set his own nets for several winters.

ABOUT THE AUTHOR

Bob Ojala's books include:

- Autobiography of a Ship's marine Surveyor
- World Travels & Adventures of a Ship's Marine Surveyor (Autobiographical)
- Sweetwater Sailors (non-fiction, real-life stories from Great Lakes mariners)
- Sweetwater Sailors – The Rest of the Story (Wives, women sailors, and "Unusual" sailors stories)
- A Tugboater's Life (Contemporary Romance based upon Great Lakes Marine Construction)
- The Tugboater Family (stand-alone, but flowing characters from A Tugboater's Life)
- Crew's Ship Affairs (Life on a large cruise ship, BELOW the passenger decks)
- KIDNAPPED – A Tugboater's Tale (Human Trafficking in middle-America)
- UNDERCOVER AGAIN – Fighting Human Trafficking
-

www.ingramcontent.com/pod-product-compliance
Lightning Source LLC
Chambersburg PA
CBHW060422010526
44118CB00017B/2327